*"You know, I just
paint the thing I see
the way I feel it. I
have no particular
theories. I just try
to paint well."*

TUNIS PONSEN

The Lost Paintings of Tunis Ponsen
(1891-1968)

This exhibition was organized by the

MUSKEGON MUSEUM OF ART

with support provided by

CITIZENS INSURANCE COMPANY OF AMERICA

Contributing Authors

WILLIAM H. GERDTS
Professor of Art History
Graduate School of the City University of New York

SUSAN S. WEININGER
Associate Professor of Art History
Roosevelt University, Chicago, Illinois

PATRICK COFFEY
Vice President – Marketing
Citizens Insurance Company of America

KENNETH KATZ
Conservation and Museum Services
Detroit, Michigan

The Lost Paintings of Tunis Ponsen
(1891-1968)

Muskegon Museum of Art
Muskegon, Michigan
SEPTEMBER 11 - NOVEMBER 27, 1994

Kalamazoo Institute of Arts
Kalamazoo, Michigan
APRIL 1 - MAY 14, 1995

Dennos Museum Centre
Traverse City, Michigan
JUNE 11 - AUGUST 27, 1995

Flint Institute of Arts
Flint, Michigan
SEPTEMBER 24 - NOVEMBER 19, 1995

Kresge Art Museum
Michigan State University
East Lansing, Michigan
JANUARY 8 - MARCH 17, 1996

Harold Washington Library Center
Chicago, Illinois
JUNE 29 - AUGUST 24, 1996

Sage Center for the Arts
Hillsdale College
Hillsdale, Michigan
SEPTEMBER 3 - 29, 1996

CATALOGUE DESIGN: Sheila B. Warners
TYPOGRAPHY: Graphics Unlimited
PRINTING: Custom Service Printers, Inc.
CATALOGUE PRODUCTION: Melissa A. Freye

COVER: **YACHT CLUB PIER**
Collection of Muskegon Museum of Art
Gift of Friends of Art
Accession 31.3
Photography by Larry Dikeman

TABLE OF CONTENTS

Acknowledgements 6
HENRY MATTHEWS

The Lost Paintings of Tunis Ponsen 8
PATRICK COFFEY

Introduction: Tunis Ponsen Discovered 10
DR. WILLIAM H. GERDTS

Tunis Ponsen 18
SUSAN S. WEININGER

Chronology 36
PATRICK COFFEY

Color Plates and Reference 56

Technical Conservation of Ponsen's Works 104
KENNETH B. KATZ

Figure Illustration References 110

Authors' Biographies 112

ACKNOWLEDGEMENTS

BY HENRY MATTHEWS

INTERIM DIRECTOR,

CURATOR OF COLLECTIONS AND EXHIBITIONS

MUSKEGON MUSEUM OF ART

For the Muskegon Museum of Art, *The Lost Paintings of Tunis Ponsen* represents the culmination of a long association with the artist. Shortly after his arrival in Michigan from his native Holland, Ponsen attended art classes in this museum, then known as the Hackley Art Gallery. With the encouragement of gallery director Lulu Miller, he continued his studies at the School of the Art Institute in Chicago, returning to Muskegon for several one-person exhibitions over the course of his life.

In 1931, the Friends of Art purchased *Yacht Club Pier* (cat. #11) from Ponsen's fifth one-person exhibition at the Hackley Art Gallery, as a gift for the gallery's permanent collection. Its inherent strength and beauty, coupled with the historic significance relative to this museum, led us to select *Yacht Club Pier* as the signature image for the exhibition. It appears on the catalogue cover and exhibition poster.

Over the years, Ponsen exhibited his work many times at the Hackley Art Gallery, concluding with the final one-person exhibit of his career just months before he died in 1968.

This *Tunis Ponsen* exhibition also represents an exceptionally fortuitous series of events that allowed us the privilege of rediscovering Ponsen's works. Angenita J. Morris, Ponsen's only living relative, played a unique role. Together with her late husband, Ken, Angenita carefully cared for Ponsen's vast body of work along with invaluable archival materials from his long career. Their devotion and steadfast determination preserved Ponsen's paintings and created the opportunity for us to rediscover the artist's expressive *oeuvre*.

The extraordinary body of Ponsen's work came to the attention of Citizens Insurance Company through the Morrises' application for homeowner's insurance coverage. Patrick Coffey, Citizens' vice president-marketing, and member of the Appraisers Association of America, with an extensive background in art history, was called in as a consultant. He was immediately captivated by the power of Ponsen's work, convinced it merited the attention of the scholastic community and the museum public.

Led by Ponsen's early artistic roots here at the Hackley Gallery, Coffey began a dialogue with then-

MMA director Al Kochka, and myself, to explore the concept of an exhibition of paintings by Tunis Ponsen.

The initial concept of an exhibit grew to include substantial scholarly research, a major publication and a tour of museums throughout Michigan and Chicago— all made possible through the generous support of Citizens Insurance Company of America. Coffey's interest in Ponsen's works has been steadfast and complete, and we are indebted to him for his unwavering encouragement, support and dedication.

An exhibition is, first and foremost, a body of works of art. However, without interpretation and critical scrutiny, there is little meaning beyond the beauty of the surface. Two distinguished scholars of American art have shared their critical insights on Tunis Ponsen. Dr. William H. Gerdts, leading authority on American Impressionism, is a critically acclaimed author, lecturer and professor at the Graduate School of the City University of New York. His contribution to this catalogue is an articulate and insightful essay, placing Tunis Ponsen in the larger context of modern American painting of the first half of this century.

Susan S. Weininger, lecturer and author on Modernism and the Chicago art scene, contributed a scholarly and accessible essay placing Tunis Ponsen in the context of the vastly divergent Chicago milieu. Weininger, a Ph.D. candidate at the University of Chicago, is Associate Professor and Director of the Art Division of the School of Liberal Studies at Roosevelt University. As curator of a number of significant exhibitions in Chicago, she has published important articles and catalogue essays which have helped reshape our knowledge of the Chicago art scene in the first half of this century.

"The Lost Paintings of Tunis Ponsen invites us to rediscover a gentle, yet powerful painter who made a significant contribution to the Chicago art scene…"

Citizens' corporate support also enabled us to provide special conservation treatment and reframing of the works selected for this exhibition. Kenneth B. Katz of Conservation and Museum Services and Raymond Anderson Framing employed great technical expertise as they analyzed, assessed and restored the paintings and their frames, returning them to the artist's original intent.

Special thanks are in order for a dedicated museum staff including Registrar Babs Vaughan and Public Relations/Publications Coordi- nator Melissa Freye whose numerous contributions far exceeded job descriptions. Thanks also to Sheila Wright and Peter Logan of Citizens Insurance Company for their patient and very helpful assistance.

For collectors, it can be a great inconvenience to be without their "treasures" for months, or even years, as their work of art travels with an exhibition. Angenita Morris generously opened her collection and shared its gems with us through this exhibition. I also wish to thank Pamela and Harlan Berk and Powell Bridges, whose loans represent important Ponsen paintings that add a significant dimension to the exhibition.

The Lost Paintings of Tunis Ponsen invites us to rediscover a gentle, yet powerful painter who made a significant contribution to the Chicago art scene of the 1920s through 1940s. We enjoy this opportunity as the result of Angenita J. Morris' lifelong dedication and the generous support of Citizens Insurance Company of America. I would like to express our deepest appreciation to Angenita for sharing Ponsen's works with the museum world and to Citizens Insurance Company whose leadership and commitment to excellence set the standard for this entire undertaking.

-H.M.

THE LOST PAINTINGS
OF TUNIS PONSEN

BY PATRICK COFFEY

VICE PRESIDENT – MARKETING

CITIZENS INSURANCE COMPANY OF AMERICA

This fascinating story begins in the summer of 1990 when Michigan residents Mr. & Mrs. H. Kenneth Morris submitted an application for a homeowner's insurance policy to Citizens Insurance Company of America headquartered in Howell, Michigan. Because the application requested fine arts insurance on 110 paintings and watercolors by an artist named Tunis Ponsen, the Citizens underwriter reviewing the application asked my opinion of them. I happen to be a certified fine arts appraiser and member of the Appraisers Association of America, New York, so I occasionally serve as a fine arts consultant to Citizens underwriters.

While I had heard the name Tunis Ponsen before, I knew virtually nothing about him or his work. I discovered that he is included in the major dictionaries of American artists and even in the leading dictionary of world artists published in France, *Dictionnaire des Peintres, Sculpteurs* by E. Benezit (Librairie Grund 1976).

I learned that Tunis Ponsen was born in the Netherlands in 1891, emigrated to America in 1913, lived in Muskegon, Michigan until 1925, and then moved to Chicago where he became an important regional artist. I also learned that he had become a largely forgotten artist even before his death in 1968 and that, for some unknown reason, his works only rarely appeared on the art markets.

Because of my concern about the physical condition of so many paintings, I arranged a visit to the Morris home in the fall of 1990. There my wife and I met Angenita and Ken Morris, who proved to be a delightful couple in their retirement years.

We simply were not prepared for the dazzling array of very fine quality oil paintings and watercolors that greeted our eyes when we first entered the Morris home. There were portraits, Chicago scenes, landscapes, still lifes and even some New England harbor scenes. I commented to the Morrises that I had no idea that Tunis Ponsen was such a skilled painter and that I couldn't understand why his work wasn't better known.

Every single room on the main floor was hung with Tunis Ponsen paintings. When we finished there, Angenita Morris took us downstairs to a completed lower level where it was more of the same, a seemingly endless array of fine paintings.

We had just turned to start back upstairs when Angenita said, "There is one more room that you might like to see." She opened a closed door and invited us to step inside. We both stood there in awe as though we had stumbled into King Solomon's mines! There, in front of our eyes, were literally hundreds and hundreds of paintings and watercolors, all neatly stacked in wooden storage racks.

When I inquired how many there might be, Angenita said, "Oh, somewhere around 1,000." I thought to myself, "No wonder Tunis Ponsen's work so rarely appears on the art markets. It's all stored here in a house in Michigan!"

Angenita went on to explain that she was Tunis Ponsen's niece and had been his sole heir at the time of his death in 1968. She and Ken began a series of weekly trips to the artist's large Chicago home. Each visit, they would load as many paintings as would fit into their car and carried them back to their Michigan home. After many such trips, they finally rented a trailer and completed the task in the summer of 1968.

Angenita Morris was determined to restore the name and work of her uncle to a place of prominence in the art world. As she would later put it, "I had this dream to find a way somehow to make people aware that there was a Tunis Ponsen who had a special talent and who left behind some very memorable paintings."

To keep that dream alive, she resolved not to hold a large liquidation auction. Instead, Ken constructed a

We simply were not prepared for the dazzling array of very fine quality oil paintings and watercolors that greeted our eyes when we first entered the Morris home.

series of sturdy storage racks in the lower level of their home. Except for what they hung on their walls, all of the remaining art was placed in the separate storage room which was provided with year-round controlled temperature and humidity. As a result of this careful attention, the passing of more than 25 years finds their physical condition to be excellent.

Two more visits to the Morris home in 1991 confirmed my early impression that Tunis Ponsen's body of work really merited more recognition than it had previously received. Because his first American roots had been in Muskegon, I contacted the Muskegon Museum of Art to inquire if any of their staff might be interested in a visit to the Morris home.

They were, indeed. In February, 1992, then-director, Al Kochka and Curator of Collections and Exhibitions Henry Matthews, viewed the Tunis Ponsen estate for themselves. They both shared my enthusiasm for Ponsen's work and expressed an interest in organizing a traveling museum exhibition.

Citizens' management viewed this as an opportunity to add to the broad range of other public-spirited programs which it sponsors and has provided the funding which has made the current exhibition possible.

While Ken Morris has not lived to share it with her, Angenita Morris' 25-year dream has become a reality. As the last major exhibition of Tunis Ponsen's work occurred in 1938, most of these artworks have been largely unknown for more than a half century. Citizens Insurance Company is proud to play a role in bringing this exciting discovery to public attention.

– P.C.

9

TUNIS PONSEN DISCOVERED

BY WILLIAM H. GERDTS

PROFESSOR OF ART HISTORY

GRADUATE SCHOOL OF THE

CITY UNIVERSITY OF NEW YORK

When Patrick Coffey, whom I'd met some time back in connection with the work of the American Impressionist painter, Theodore Robinson, got in touch with me over a year ago concerning the paintings of Tunis Ponsen, I was introduced to an artist about whom I'd heretofore been completely ignorant. Though unlike a good many art historians here in the East, I have long been interested in artistic developments throughout the United States– that was the subject of my longest (and heaviest) book, the three-volume *Art Across America*, published in 1990. Ponsen was an artist with whose work I had not crossed paths. This may be, in part at least – and this is, anyway, my rationale – that my study extended from whatever beginnings existed in each state and region to about 1920, and Ponsen's professional career really begins just beyond that date.

Still, as an historian of American painting and sculpture, my interests continue to more recent times. Ponsen's obscurity and neglect, after all, extends even to those areas of the near-Midwest with which he was professionally associated – western Michigan and Chicago. Even in his own period of greatest artistic activity, he was hardly a household name; Ponsen was omitted in J. Z. Jacobson's *Art of Today Chicago – 1933* (actually copyrighted in 1932). This may be explained by the fact that many of the artists with whom Jacobson dealt were involved with more modernist concerns (though a Modernism considerably weakened from that of their European forebears) than those with which Ponsen was involved. But even among the over-one hundred contemporary Chicago artists profiled by the critic, Clarence J. Bulliet, for his series on "Artists of Chicago Past & Present" which appeared in the *Chicago Daily News* in the mid-1930s, and which ran the range from relatively conservative and Impressionist painters to those espousing modernist concerns, Ponsen was neglected.

The explanation for such an omission is probably complex, involving both Ponsen's limited public, institutional, and commercial exposure, along with the climate and even ferment of the art worlds, both national and Chicago-local, during the 1920s and after, and involving the tug-of-war between traditionalists and modernists. This struggle – and Ponsen's place within it – would be the province of a more regionally specialized art historian than myself, and I would rather devote this essay to my own observations of the artist's paintings.

First, though, a word or two about Regional American painting. American art history, whether as taught in our colleges and universities, presented in our major museums, acquired by collectors with a preference for their national heritage, or offered for sale in commercial galleries, has tended to concentrate upon art produced by painters and sculptors of the Northeast, centering upon Boston, Philadelphia, and especially New York City. This is true wherever the schools, the institutions, the private collectors, and the dealers are located.

Now, there are increasing signs of change here. In some regions, some states, some cities, interest in their own heritage has indeed developed over the past decade or two, but very unevenly. California is now extremely conscious and proud of its artistic heritage in its several geographic centers, north and south. This has spilled over to the extent that a number of New York galleries have shown work by California Impressionists, and the major auction galleries are just now beginning to present groups of California pictures together as a special section within their semi-annual major American auctions. Elsewhere, there has been a thriving concern in Indiana for the work of Indiana artists, and likewise in Cincinnati, Ohio, in recognition of that city's heritage. But elsewhere in the Midwest, regional pride has been surprisingly weak, with the Detroit Institute of Arts just recently selling off a large group of fine paintings by leading Michigan artists of the past. In Chicago, despite a long, strong, and very individual artistic tradition going back to the 1850s – a richer and more varied tradition than exists for Indianapolis, for instance – the major art institutions have left the investigation of Illinois painting and sculpture to the history museums– the Chicago Historical Society, along with the Illinois State Museum in Springfield. But there are hopeful signs here, too, with a few commercial galleries now showing interest in Chicago's artistic tradition and at least one major private collection formed of the work of the Illinois Impressionists.

There is no reason to believe that Tunis Ponsen's artistic career integrated with the rather sparse professional artistic tradition that existed in Muskegon, Michigan, in the early twentieth century, where Victor Casenelli, a painter of landscapes and Native American subjects was the leading resident painter. Yet, it would seem unlikely that Ponsen would have been unfamiliar with the Ox-Bow Summer School of Art in nearby Saugatuck, which had formed an association with the Art Institute of Chicago only a few years before Ponsen entered the Institute in 1924. It is in Chicago, primarily, that Ponsen's regional associations should be established.

During my first exposure to Ponsen's pictures, those which struck me most forcibly, both in terms of the power of the imagery and also their high degree of artistry, were his urban scenes.

During my first exposure to Ponsen's pictures, those which struck me most forcibly, both in terms of the power of the imagery and also their high degree of artistry, were his urban scenes. These, actually are of several kinds, but I was most taken by those which dramatized the Chicago skyline, pictures such as *Chicago River Industrial Scene* (cat. #25), and especially *Chicago Silhouettes* (cat. #24). A year ago I was immersed in writing a study of the New York imagery created by

American Impressionist painters such as Childe Hassam, Colin Campbell Cooper, and others, who devoted much of their achievement to glorifying the modern city, and locating the touchstone of such imagery in the skyscraper.

Now, one thinks of modern architectural construction and the skyscraper as a contribution even more associated with Chicago than New York City, but I have come across far fewer such images of Chicago's buildings and its skyline than those celebrating New York. Of course, both my regional purview and my Impressionist focus here was on the first two decades of the twentieth century, but during this period there appears to have been relatively little visual imagery in Chicago devoted to recent urban changes – no pictorial equivalent of the East Coast celebration of "The New New York." The Chicago artist I most associate with such subject matter was the French-born and trained Albert Fleury, who arrived in that city in 1888 to paint landscapes for the Chicago Auditorium, and stayed on as an instructor at the Art Institute while recording the streets, new skyscrapers, and other landmark buildings, as well as the commercial life of the Chicago waterfront. Indeed, Fleury may be considered the precursor of Ponsen in this phase of the latter's artistic production.

Fleury's painting, though, was very much of its time. Animated by vibrant, broken brushstrokes which translated into sparkling street lights, reflecting windows, and swirling steam clouds, and peopled by myriad small pedestrians, his art was the Midwest equivalent of Hassam's and Cooper's. Ponsen's urban images, created a generation later, make use of simplified architectural forms, stylized, soaring silhouettes, and the reduction of these images into semi-abstract, geometric shapes, which bring to mind the 1920s paintings of the Precisionists, and especially, perhaps, the New York scenes of Georgia O'Keeffe. The best-known of these paintings of O'Keeffe are close-up views of one or two buildings, but more akin to Ponsen's pictures are those glowing scenes looking across the East River from the Shelton Hotel, painted by O'Keeffe in 1926-28, such as *East River No. 3* (Vassar College Art Gallery, Poughkeepsie), and *East River from the 20th Story of the Shelton Hotel* (New Britain Museum of

American Art). Ponsen's marvellous *Chicago Silhouettes* shares with these paintings even the neutral tonalities of grey and black which lend a faint melancholy to the drama of modern architectural forms. Likewise, Ponsen's silvery sky and its reflection in the broad planes of the Chicago River harmoniously balances natural forms with the man-made modernist buildings, similar in treatment to O'Keeffe's. Ponsen's is an ideal city of the future, seen soaring high in the distance beyond the darker horizontal planes of foreground and industrial bridge.

O'Keeffe's urban images are perhaps the closest Precisionist analogues to this phase of Ponsen's art, but other Eastern painters may provide alternative comparisons. Earlier than O'Keeffe's images were Stefan Hirsch's 1921 *New York, Lower Manhattan* (Phillips Collection, Washington, D. C.) and Louis Lozowick's *Chicago* (private collection, Washington, D. C.) of 1923, though the latter was one of Lozowick's "City" series originally painted in Berlin, (the series subsequently replicated back in the United States), rather than in the American heartland, while Lozowick's jarring distortions – flattened forms surrounding a tunnel vision-rush through the piled-up geometric masses – contrasts with Ponsen's more naturalistic treatment of space. Other Chicago painters, too, created works celebrating urban optimism with skyscraper imagery prior to Ponsen, such as Raymond Jonson with his 1921 *The Night – Chicago* (fig. 1), but the following year Jonson began to paint in New Mexico and in 1924 he moved there permanently, so that he would seem to have offered little inspiration for Ponsen. A more enduring and forceful figure in the Chicago art world during the 1920s was Rudolph Weisenborn, but his modernism was far more extreme than Ponsen's; his 1928 *Chicago* (Illinois State Museum) completely abstracted the urban imagery beyond recognition in a powerful, nonobjective composition. In the 1930s, Frank Sohn was a Chicago painter who sometimes interpreted urban imagery, but his art was rooted in more Post-Impressionist traditions.

Among Ponsen's teachers at the Art Institute – the Impressionist figure painter, Karl Buehr, the landscape painter, George Oberteuffer, and the New York artist,

Leon Kroll – it was the last who may have had the greatest impact in regard to urban imagery, for Kroll had devoted a good deal of his time during the 1910s to modernist scenes of New York City. A good many of these, such as *Lower New York – the Bridge in Winter* (Tulsa City Library) and *Building New York* (Irving Mitchell Felt), both of 1915, bear similarities to Ponsen's works, although by the mid-1920s, when he was teaching in Chicago, Kroll had turned away from such imagery to concentrate on the figure, often nude, and on Cézanne-like landscape settings. One wonders if Ponsen had any affiliation with Anthony Angarola, an influential, moderately modernist Chicago artist of the 'twenties, who was both a figure and scene painter, and as Susan S. Weininger has written, "emphasized the abstract potential of the colors and shapes in the urban landscape." Weininger quoted Angarola in regard to the Halsted Street Bridge: "It appeals to me because of straight majestic lines....As it soars above the old boats moving below, the background of the bridge serves splendidly," a comment which suggests a close sympathy with Ponsen's approach to urban images. Angarola was extremely influential as a teacher at the Art Institutes in both Chicago and Kansas City; Frank Sohn was one of his pupils, and he was a close friend of the important Chicago painter, William S. Schwartz. who prepared studies for a modernist urban mural, *Modern Transportation of Mail* (never executed) in 1932, which also bears comparison with several of Ponsen's Chicago images. Unfortunately, Angarola died in 1929 at the age of thirty-six. Of all his Chicago contemporaries, though, it was probably Richard Chase whose paintings bear the closest comparison with this phase of Ponsen's art – see, for instance, Chase's *Copper and Steel* (Valparaiso University Museum of Art, Indiana) – and such a comparison offers validity to the pairing of Ponsen and Chase at several exhibitions held at the Chicago Art Galleries before and after 1930. Chase, in fact, who, like Ponsen, was a pupil of Karl Buehr, though a portraitist by profession, created a "Portrait of Chicago Over a Ten-Year Period" in a series of urban canvases during the 1920s and '30s.

Actually, only a few of Ponsen's pictures shown here are paeans to urban Modernism, though the artist

Fig. 1 – Raymond Jonson. *The Night – Chicago.*

Fig. 2 – Anthony Angarola. *Michigan Avenue Bridge – Chicago River.*

Fig. 3 – Ramon Shiva. *Chicago MCMXXIV*, 1924.

Fig. 4 – Emil Armin. *The Open Bridge*

Fig. 5 – John Steuart Curry. *Wisconsin Landscape*, 1938-39

certainly painted others; his *Castles of Today*, exhibited in 1931 at Art Institute in the Annual Exhibition of Works by Artists of Chicago and Vicinity, must certainly be such a picture. But other of his urban scenes concentrate rather upon machine forms and urban industry and activity, pictures that also bear an alliance with the Precisionists of the 1920s such as Charles Sheeler, and which ally Ponsen with many of the leading Chicago painters of that decade such as Angarola (see his *Michigan Avenue Bridge – Chicago River*, fig. 2), Ramon Shiva (as in *Chicago MCMXXIV*, fig. 3), Emil Thulin, who painted industrial scenes enveloped in a more vibrating, somewhat Impressionist manner (as in his 1939 *Steel Mills, South Chicago*, Valparaiso University Museum of Art, Indiana); and even the more consciously primitivizing Emil Armin (*The Open Bridge*, c. 1930, fig. 4). Richard Chase again comes to mind here; see his *Tough Stuff* (Valparaiso University Museum of Art, Indiana). But the recognition and even glorification of industry and the machine was not a local but rather a national phenomenon, prevalent throughout the industrialized sections of the country during the 1920s through the '40s. Following the lead of Charles Sheeler in documenting the technological landscape at the Ford Motor Company's River Rouge Plant near Detroit in 1927, grain elevators were featured by numerous Buffalo painters of the period, for instance, such as Charles Burchfield and Arthur Lindberg, and even in Halifax, Nova Scotia, by a group of talented women painters, Marion Bond, Edith Smith, and Elizabeth Styring Nutt, while steel mills were emphasized in pictures by Pittsburgh's Aaron Gorson, Cleveland's August Biehle, Detroit's Zoltan Sepeshy, and Milwaukee's Edmund Lewandowski, as well as by Chicago's Raymond Perry in Johnstown, Pennsylvania and by William Schwartz, probably in Gary, Indiana.

Even more of Ponsen's urban scenes are of local streets and alleyways, such as *Rainy Day* (cat. # 33), *Demolition in Hyde Park* (cat. #40), *House on Oakenwald* (cat. #35), *Heavy Snow* (cat. #39), and *Snow in Chicago Alley* (cat. #36). Some of these, painted in dark neutral tones such as the last-named, with its claustrophobic enclosure of dark structures on either side, are purposefully melancholic, reflective of the depression era, and very much a part of the current American Scene painting of the 1930s. They are not unlike some of Burchfield's pictures of the period painted in and around Buffalo, such as his *Ice Glare* (Whitney Museum of American Art) of 1933, and share a somewhat similar aesthetic and theme with Chicago's Jean Crawford Adams. Even closer are some of the urban scenes of Scottish-born James Jeffrey Grant, who arrived in Chicago in 1907 and established a painting studio there in 1920. Works by Grant such as *In the Old Neighborhood* (Valparaiso University Museum of Art, Indiana) recall Ponsen's *Snow in Chicago Alley;* these pictures, unlike the paintings featuring Chicago's panoramic skyline, emphasize the anonymity of big city life, stressing rather the neighborhood – the part, rather than the whole – made somehow even more personal and wistful with their mantels of snow. Ponsen's Parisian paintings, too, such as *A Street in Paris* (cat. #20) and *Barges on the Seine* (cat. #21), though they certainly capture a sense of specific place, avoid the touristic for the neighborhood.

That anonymity extends to Ponsen's pictures of scenes of small towns, such as his *Country Train Station* (cat. #30) and *Midwest Backyards* (cat #29); the latter could in fact, be located either in Chicago or western Michigan, or very possibly a town such as Galena, where Ponsen painted a number of strong canvases such as *Galena, Illinois* (cat. #28), *Wash Day, Galena, Illinois,* and *Downtown, Galena, Illinois.* These are, in some ways, the artist's pictures which most accord with the dominant "American Scene" aesthetic of the period, and where much American painting reflects traditional values, both aesthetic and cultural, quite separate from the urban issues dominant in New York City. In pictures such as these, Ponsen delights in the variety of architectural shapes and masses, carefully aligned with their natural settings, and only distantly reflecting the geometry of Modernism. This was a genre to be found throughout the Midwest in the 1920s and '30s; comparable work, for instance, was produced by Milwaukee's Gustave Moeller with his *Main Street, Alma* (Milwaukee Journal Gallery of Wisconsin Art) of 1926.

Ponsen's pure landscapes vary considerably in their associations. Given his origins and early years spent in The Netherlands, it is not surprising that his Dutch landscapes, such as *Backyards of My Childhood* (cat. #18) and *Windmill near Delft* (cat. #19), suggest the strong tradition of plein-air landscape painting in that country during the late nineteenth century, though Ponsen's pictures were created in 1928 when he was able to return to his native land with the award of the Bryant Lathrop Traveling Scholarship from the Art Institute of Chicago. The windmill is a motif usually associated with Holland, and one that figures strongly in the work of The Hague School, the group of late nineteenth century Dutch painters of landscapes and rural life which included Hendrik Mesdag, Anton Mauve, and the three Maris Brothers. But Ponsen's Dutch paintings also emphasize the flat terrain and rustic, often empty countryside, as well as a sense of visual intimacy which were featured in the paintings of that most celebrated group of Dutch artists still active during his early years in the Netherlands. On the other hand, Ponsen's *Apple Tree* (cat. #37) suggests a lingering homage to the Post-Impressionist, Vincent Van Gogh, (also, significantly, a Dutch painter) while Expressionist overtones can be found in his treatment of *An Old Tree* (cat. #38). But it seems to me that one of Ponsen's most powerful paintings of all is his *Midwest Landscape with Storm* (cat. #31), which places him firmly in the tradition of the Midwestern Regionalist movement. Here, the breadth of the countryside and the artist's ability to effect real tension from casually mundane topography through his manipulation of light, shade, and color, capturing the effect of imminent natural drama, recalls especially the contemporaneous paintings of the Regionalists, Grant Wood, Thomas Hart Benton, and John Steuart Curry, above all Curry's *Spring Shower* (Metropolitan Museum of Art, New York City), of 1931, a Kansas scene; his *Line Storm* (private collection) of 1934; and especially Curry's magnificent *Wisconsin Landscape* (fig. 5) of 1938-39. Many of Ponsen's pure landscapes such as *Michigan Farm* and *Rolling Landscape, Southern Michigan* were painted in the vicinity of Benton Harbor, Michigan, where he summered during most of the 1930s.

Sadly, we know very little of Ponsen's social intimacies with other artists, in Chicago or elsewhere, beyond his friendship with his student, Ethel Crouch

Brown, but his work was combined with that of Louis Oscar Griffith and Richard Chase at the Chicago Art Galleries in the autumn of 1929; in 1934 with Chase again, along with C. Curry Bohm and Arthur Grover Rider; in 1939 with Charles W. Dahlgreen and Ruth Van Sickle Ford; in 1941 with Macena Barton and William Hollingsworth, Jr.; and in 1950 with John Bacus. Although some of these artists also dealt with the figure and occasionally still life, the majority of these painters specialized primarily in landscape and urban scenes, suggesting that this was the theme with which Ponsen was most associated during his lifetime, an identification supported by critical approval and awards. While none of these artists are shining lights in the firmament of twentieth century American painting, a number of them – Griffith, Dahlgreen, and Bohm especially– were among the leading landscapists in the Midwest at the time and provided worthy company for Ponsen and his paintings.

All three of these con- temporaries of Ponsen were associated with summer art colonies in the nation's heart- land – all of them worked in Brown County, Indiana, while Bohm was also active in the Smokies and Dahlgreen in both Saugatuck, Michigan and in the Missouri Ozarks – but Ponsen does not seem to have been drawn to such artistically popular settings. Instead, he chose Eastern art colonies for his summer outings as varied as possible from his Midwestern environment, working on the New England coast at Provincetown in 1926, at Gloucester as early as 1927, and also at Boothbay Harbor in Maine in 1930; he returned to Gloucester in 1938. Some of the work produced in these settlements were among Ponsen's most successful, judging by critical acclaim. In some

"...as I have studied his oeuvre, I have become more and more attracted to his studio interiors... These constitute, it seems to me perhaps, the artist's most individual works..."

ways they are also among his most traditional, given the popularity of coastal harbor scenes, especially on Cape Ann, Massachusetts, all the way back to Fitz Hugh Lane in the 1840s. Ponsen's concentration on the harbors and wharfs with their activity of shipbuilding and fishing recall particularly the paintings of earlier Midwestern-born artists at Gloucester at the turn-of- the-century, painters such as Frank Duveneck and John Twachtman, as well as other Impressionists including Childe Hassam and Willard Metcalf. Indeed, Ponsen's *Gloucester Harbor* (cat. #17), with its exploration of the unusual topography of the area, is especially close to Metcalf's *Gloucester Harbor* (Mead Art Museum, Amherst College, Massachusetts) of 1895 and Hassam's *Gloucester Harbor* (Norton Gallery, West Palm Beach, Florida) of 1899-1909, and especially, in its more solid handling of the shapes of buildings and docks, to Duveneck's *Yellow Pier Shed and Gloucester Harbor From Banner Hill* (private collection) of about 1905-10. Among Chicago painters, Charles Corwin, Duveneck and Twachtman's old colleague from their years studying in Munich, joined them in Gloucester at the turn-of-the- century, continuing to summer there for many years, while two of Ponsen's teachers, Leon Kroll and George Oberteuffer, both painted there, Kroll in 1912 and again for several summers in the mid-1930s. It may have been Oberteuffer who induced Ponsen to the several coastal communities where he painted during the summers, since he also painted in both Provincetown (at the same time Ponsen was studying with him) and in Boothbay Harbor. But Ponsen's summer paintings of New England harbors are nearly identical with those painted by a host of professional artists contemporary with him, who annually summered in Gloucester and Rockport, Massachusetts.

For the most part, then, Ponsen was a painter of outdoor scenes, but not entirely so. His art developed during the 1920s when there was a general return to the studio among American artists, after many decades of concentration upon out-of-doors painting, and Ponsen joined in the exploration of more defined subject matter in a controlled environment. This included the painting of a good many formal still lifes such as his *Arrangement with Eggs* (cat. #6), a "kitchen" still life which bespeaks the tradition of the much-heralded Emil Carlsen in the decades before and after 1900, and ultimately derives from the revival of admiration for the work of the great eighteenth-century French painter, Jean Baptiste Simeon Chardin. But Ponsen's heritage from more modern concerns can be found here in his fascination with the perfect ovoid forms of the small eggs, contrasted with the open, circular void of the metal cooking pot from which they issue, along with that of the hard, upright tankard and the soft, sinuous vegetables laid out horizontally on the table top.

Another aspect of Ponsen's concern with more formal and traditional subject matter are his portraits and figure studies. The formal portraits, such as that of Katharine Cornell, are able enough pictures, but he is more interesting, I think, in his character studies, from the *Young Man with Violin* (cat. #3) and *Study of a Young Woman* (cat. #4), to his vivid presentations of old age, as in his *Seated Old Man with Cane* (cat. #8) and his *Portrait of Man in a Black Hat* (cat. #7). The last-named, especially, in its sharp silhouette, its simplified forms, and its strong tonal contrasts remind me of the marvellous figure studies painted in Chicago during the 1910s by Raymond Jonson, William Penhallow Henderson, and Bror J. O. Nordfeldt, before they left the Midwest, the first two for Santa Fe and Nordfeldt for New York and Provincetown, though he, too, wound up in Santa Fe, through Henderson's persuasion. These were among the most distinctive figure paintings created in the United States in the early twentieth century and something of their combination of perceptive realism with the strategies of modernism inform Ponsen's pictures.

I began my discussion of Ponsen's art by expressing my initial admiration for his pictures of modern Chicago; but as I have studied his oeuvre, I have become more and more attracted to his studio interiors – *An Open Door* (cat. #47), *Room with Red Drop Leaf Table* (cat. #46), *Red Drop Leaf Table with Bottles* (cat. #45), *The Japanese Vase* (cat. #43) and *Still Life with Sansevieria* (cat. #44). These constitute, it seems to me perhaps, the artist's most individual works, this beyond the fact that they represent, of course, his own personal and artistic environment. They speak of Ponsen's art, his own pictures, such as the Cornell portrait on the wall, and his artistic preferences, such as the book open to a reproduction of a work by Van Gogh. As much as his own series of Self-Portraits, these are also portraits of the artist – a painter factual and straight forward, object-oriented, but a "no-frills" fellow, and concerned with his craft. Rooms penetrate one into the other, suggesting the continuum of his own life style, though what might be mysterious or ominous, as in the painted interiors of Ponsen's Cedar Rapids, Iowa, contemporary, Marvin Cone, is made cheerful and inviting by him through the sunny illumination and rich chromaticism – the brightest range of color of any of Ponsen's pictures. Other painters of the period, whose room interiors share qualities with Ponsen's include Nicolai Cikovsky, whose *Still Life with Self-Portrait* (private collection) of 1938 includes brightly defined furniture, along with one of his own pictures of himself on the wall, and Charles Burchfield, whose *Pussy Willows* (Munson-Williams-Proctor Institute, Utica, New York) combines a still life in the room with a view out the studio window, not unlike Ponsen's *The Japanese Vase*. Such paintings describe the artist's life, and they describe the artist, too.

– W.G.

TUNIS PONSEN

BY SUSAN S. WEININGER

ASSOCIATE PROFESSOR OF ART HISTORY

ROOSEVELT UNIVERSITY

CHICAGO, ILLINOIS

Like many other Chicago artists, Tunis Ponsen has been largely overlooked by scholars of 20th century art. With the possible exception of Ivan Albright, until fairly recently it would have been difficult for even those educated in the arts to name a Chicago artist who was active before 1965. During the last decade, however, a series of exhibitions and publications has focused on the unknown artists of the early part of the century and has generated interest in these artists. We can now add William S. Schwartz, Emil Armin, Julia Thecla, Gertrude Abercrombie, Belle Baranceanu, Anthony Angarola, Kathleen Blackshear, Raymond Jonson, Manierre Dawson, Herman Menzel, William Norton, and Archibald J. Motley, Jr. to the ever-increasing group of artists whose work has been exhibited and documented.[1] These artists are, however, primarily modernists – artists who participated in the early 20th century struggle to express individual feelings or ideas in their work. One of the few contemporary publications on art, J.Z. Jacobson's 1932 book, *Art of Today: 1933*, includes many of them.[2]

Ponsen, unlike these self-defined modernists, worked primarily in a traditional manner. In addition, he aligned himself with the more moderate tendency in Chicago by exhibiting in venues that were predominantly conservative, in turn attracting critics, like Eleanor Jewett, who supported this tendency. He exhibited regularly at the Chicago Galleries Association, a moderate group, throughout his career. Because almost no attention has been given to the often very interesting and technically superb work of the more traditional of the early Chicago painters, rediscovering Ponsen is even more important.[3] As we look at his *oeuvre*, it becomes clear that he does not simply paint beautiful images, although he often does that. His abiding interest and commitment was to paint, like the Impressionists he most certainly admired, what he saw. In the subjects he treated during the course of his almost 50 year career as a painter – figure studies, portraits, still lifes and landscapes – he never strayed far from this principle. And it is the landscape, both rural and urban, that provided him with his most powerful inspiration. Beginning with his weekend painting excursions to scenic locations around Muskegon with his early teacher Wilbur Kensler, Ponsen worked outside, trying to capture effects of changing light and atmospheric conditions, often referring to the seasons, weather conditions, or time of day in the titles of his paintings. This is exemplified by one of the earliest landscapes in this exhibition, *Gray Day at Provincetown* of 1926 (cat. #10), as well as the mid-career *Midwest Landscape with Storm* (cat. #31) and the late *Heavy Snow* (cat. #39), clearly indicating the lifelong importance of these concerns.

Ponsen was not, however, inflexible. Some of his most compelling paintings, like *Chicago Silhouettes* (cat. #24), or *Chicago River Industrial Scene* (cat. #25), done in the 1930s, show strong links to Chicago's modernist tradition. A willingness to experiment is evident not only in his later attempts at abstraction (*Abstract*, cat. #50; *Sunbeams through the Clouds*, cat. #49) but also in his brilliantly colored views of his studio (for example, *An Open Door*, cat. #47), probably done in the late 1950s and 1960s. In addition, at the age of about 60, he explored the use of the newly available acrylic paints in works like *View of Chicago through Birch Trees* (cat. #48).

Tunis Ponsen can be claimed as a Chicago artist, although, like many others, he did not originate in the city. He came to Chicago to study at the School of the Art Institute of Chicago in 1924 and, like many others, never left. Chicago was attractive to Ponsen for a number of reasons – it boasted an excellent art school in relatively close proximity to his adopted home of Muskegon, Michigan and his beloved sister and her family in Benton Harbor, Michigan, it was an art center that nurtured a conservative tradition, an extension of his prior artistic experience; it was a city that was not

"His skill as an artist and lack of rigidity allowed him to bridge the gap between traditional and modern, although on balance his work came down firmly in the former camp."

daunting, but manageable, friendly, midwestern. Even before his formal education was complete, he was gaining a reputation, exhibiting a landscape called *Near the Harbor, Gloucester* (location unknown) at the prestigious juried Annual Exhibition of American Paintings and Sculpture at the Art Institute of Chicago in 1927. In the same year, he exhibited for the first time at the juried Exhibition for Michigan Artists at the Detroit Institute of Arts and the juried Exhibition by Artists of Chicago and Vicinity at the Art Institute. He began to exhibit with the South Side Art Association in 1926. He was able to support himself by selling his work, supplementing his income with part-time teaching, for the rest of his life.[4]

In 1932, a reporter for the *Christian Science Monitor* asked Tunis Ponsen if there was any special message he would like to communicate to the public about his art. According to the writer, he smiled shyly and said, "None. You know, I just paint the thing I see the way I feel it. I have no particular theories. I just try to paint well."[5] In an undated clipping of about the same time, the anonymous critic called The Previewer praises Ponsen's contribution to an exhibition at the Chicago Galleries Association, writing "I found Tunis Ponsen the outstanding Artist (with a capital A) in the show. He says he wants to paint what he sees, and he is modern in the true sense; he paints things without letting textbook rules interfere with his eyes."[6] Ponsen's natural reticence and humility made him even less prone than most artists to articulate his motives or to try to explain his paintings. In the few written comments on his work that survive, however, he reiterated these ideas: he painted what he saw and he did not follow any particular theory.[7] This attitude distinguishes him from the more vocal and rebellious group of modernists working in Chicago during the interwar period. Almost all of them discussed theory, primarily theory derived from the Russian artist-theorist Wassily Kandinsky. They valued internal expression over faithfulness to vision, as did modernists elsewhere.[8] Given his background and training, however, it is not astonishing that Ponsen followed a fairly conservative path. What is surprising is the extent to which he was open to modernist techniques. The particular climate of Chicago's art community provided Ponsen with encouragement and exhibition opportunities as a conservative along with an opportunity to explore modernism. Modernists in Chicago, unlike their New York or European counterparts, were not attracted to abstraction or to extreme experimentation in other styles, making their work much more accessible to even traditionalists. Living in Chicago offered Ponsen the opportunity to explore a variety of approaches rather than remain confined to one style and to integrate modernist techniques when it seemed appropriate to his work. In this respect, his work conforms to J. Z. Jacobson's description of a modern artist as someone who is "genuinely alive, sincere and competent."[9]

Tunis Ponsen was born in the town of Wageningen, the Netherlands, on February 19, 1891, the son of a house painter and his homemaker-seamstress wife. His early interest and achievement in art is substantiated by the diploma he was granted in 1908, certifying him to teach drawing at the elementary school level in the Netherlands. His first teachers, sculptor August Falise and landscape painter turned war cartoonist Louis Raemakers, probably instilled in the young Ponsen the beginnings of the strong habits of traditional training which were reinforced by subsequent teachers.[10]

Ponsen arrived in the United States in 1913 and by 1914 was established in Muskegon, a western Michigan city in an area settled by numerous Dutch immigrants. He went into the decorating business, which he had learned from his father, doing painting and paperhanging. By 1915, he was frequenting the Hackley Art Gallery (now the Muskegon Museum of Art), making the acquaintance of its then director, Mr. Wyer, and eventually enrolling in evening classes taught by Wilbur C. Kensler.[11] Possibly with Kensler's encouragement,

Ponsen enrolled in a six-month course in drawing at the School of the Art Institute in 1917. When his studies were completed, he applied for United States citizenship and enlisted in the army. At the end of World War I, he returned to Muskegon, to the decorating business and to the Hackley Art Gallery. It was then that he met Miss Lulu Miller, director of the gallery, who became his mentor, promising him a solo exhibition when his work was good enough. Making good on her promise, before Ponsen's permanent move to Chicago in early 1924, he was featured in a group show in 1921 followed in 1922 and 1923 by one-person exhibitions at the Hackley. The level of success he achieved as an artist in Muskegon is reflected in his numerous local portrait commissions in addition to the successful sales of landscapes, still lifes, and copies after museum pieces that were exhibited in his early shows at the gallery.[12] His lifelong relationship with the gallery culminates with the current show, but includes a retrospective exhibition in 1967 as well as one-person exhibitions in 1925, 1927 and 1931.

Lulu Miller, who not only arranged for his exhibitions in Muskegon, but reviewed them for the local paper, may have offered Ponsen the support he needed to enroll in the School of the Art Institute. When he arrived in Chicago, he took an apartment-studio in the home of Mrs. Joseph Hawley, Miller's sister. By 1934, he felt the need for a larger space and rented a studio around the corner at 1031 E. 45th Street where he also gave classes. He remained in this home, at 4422 S. Oakenwald, until 1952 when he purchased his own house-studio at 5809 Harper in the Hyde Park neighborhood of Chicago.

The dedication to visual truth was conditioned by his early training, first in Europe, later in Muskegon, and finally at the School of the Art Institute of Chicago. When Ponsen became a student at the School in 1924, it was still a bastion of conservatism. The traditional pedagogy emphasized representation of the human form and required technical mastery of drawing from anatomical models and plaster casts before life drawing was attempted. Painting was only undertaken after drawing was mastered. Students were encouraged to produce work that was not only conventionally realistic but morally uplifting. Although by the time Ponsen began his studies there were signs of rebellion among students and recent graduates, the school policies and most of the faculty were firmly entrenched in tradition.[13]

Among his teachers, most often mentioned are Leon Kroll, Karl Buehr and George Oberteuffer, the latter two staunchly conservative teachers of portrait painting.[14] A photograph of Oberteuffer's class (fig. 6) with several images of the same figure arrangement that appears in Ponsen's *Young Man with Violin* (cat. #3) is evidence that it was produced as a class project . Other works that seem to be products of traditional figure painting classes at the School of the Art Institute include *Reposing Nude* (cat. #2), *Male Model* (cat. #1), *Study of a Young Woman* (cat. #4), and *Man Holding a Bottle* (cat. #5). The dark, brownish palette, clear contours and emphasis on modelling and chiaroscuro to create a sense of three-dimensionality in each of these figures show the extent to which Ponsen absorbed the more conventional aspects of academic training. The visible, virtuoso brushwork and the reflected light playing on objects link him to artists like William Merritt Chase, possibly through one of his students, like Chicago portraitist Louis Betts.[15] Not only do these works resonate with the Dutch tradition that shaped his earliest vision, but also with his adopted heritage in America.

The romantic, exotic costume in the *Study of a Young Woman* heightens the state of revery communicated in her pose, with its tilted head and closed eyes. *Man Holding a Bottle*, on the other hand, is realistic and straightforward, complete with sun-reddened face contrasted with a chalky white forehead normally shielded from the sun. That this painting was included in the Art Institute's juried Chicago and Vicinity exhibition in 1928 attests to the popularity of this type of work in Chicago as well as the quality of Ponsen's efforts during and shortly after his student years.

Ponsen's self-portraits of the 1920s (*Self-Portrait*, 1928, cat #12, and *Self-Portrait with Cigar*, 1929, cat. #13), characterized by the same technique as the figure studies, depict Ponsen emerging from a shadowy back-ground. The canvases, brushes and other artists' tools that appear in both these paintings establish his professional identity. Yet we know little more about Ponsen; the few books scattered on a table and the flowers in a vase in the earlier work are more like still

Fig. 6 – George Oberteuffer's class, School of the Art Institute Ponsen, back row; far right.

life props than personal emblems. Ponsen seems to retreat into the darkness rather than emerge from it, leaving the viewer with a picture of a reserved and objective artist whose personality does not intrude on his images.

His late *Self-Portrait* (1964, cat. #51), done just a few years before his death, is different but not more revealing. Ponsen's head and torso emerge from a light background and are pushed up to the picture plane, dominating the image. There are no references to his occupation, no extraneous detail. Dressed in a business suit and tie, he could be a slightly rumpled, but successful, executive sitting for a corporate portrait. Perhaps secure enough in his later years to feel the overt identification as an artist was not necessary, he was still interested in the representation of what he saw above what he felt.

Arrangement with Eggs (cat. #6), a beautiful still life in the traditional mode of the 18th century artist Chardin, probably dates to the 1920s as well.[16] As a student, Ponsen won an Honorable Mention in Advanced Still Life in 1924.[17] Like the more academic figure studies, this painting relies on conventional techniques of chiaroscuro, strong contours and a brownish tonality. The simple objects are built of broad brushstrokes clearly visible to the viewer. Ponsen has placed the objects on a table that has an almost Cézannesque tilt so that the eggs and vegetables emerge from the pot as from a cornucopia. Like his later agricultural landscapes, this celebrates the bounty of the natural world.

In contrast to Buehr and Oberteuffer, who must have applauded the development of Ponsen's skills as a still life and figure painter,[18] Leon Kroll encouraged experimentation, freedom and a modernist's distrust of artistic dogma. Kroll's memoirs describe his stay in Chicago during the 1924-25 academic year as a difficult one for him. According to his rendition, he chafed at the strict rules imposed on him by the dean of the School, insisting on running his classroom in the way he desired. Kroll initiated a showdown with the dean, enlisting the support of the trustees of the Art Institute and winning the right to run his classes without interference.[19] Kroll was a New York based artist associated with the Ashcan School of urban realists, a friend of George Bellows and

John Sloan. Although he painted many images of the urban scene in the first decades of the century, much of the work he produced in Chicago was figural: "I painted people out there. I painted my wife quite a bit, and models."[20] Ponsen must have seen the exhibitions of Kroll and Bellows at the Art Institute in 1924, but evidence of their influence appears in a peripheral fashion, if at all, at this time. Both Bellows and Kroll did figure studies. The loose brushstrokes and dark palette that Bellows employed in many of his portraits may be linked to Ponsen's figure studies, but in 1924 the latter had not yet shown an interest in the urban scenes for which Bellows and Kroll were so well known. For the moment, Ponsen was concerned with much more traditional images.

Beginning in 1919, Bellows, Randall Davey and Kroll had visiting professorships at the School of the Art Institute. This was enormously important for the young modernists in Chicago who responded to the belief in freedom and pursuit of individual expression preached by the older New York artists. The freedom to experiment and follow internal dictates was like a breath of fresh air in the stifling atmosphere of the School. Although the modernists and traditionalists were often at odds with one another in Chicago, they shared the conservative training of the School of the Art Institute and the generally conservative aura of the artistic community. This, and the fact that Chicago artists were operating away from the center of the art world (New York and Europe), allowed more cross-over between the groups than one might see elsewhere. Ponsen was an artist who produced, exhibited and sold both traditional Impressionist-derived landscapes and powerful, simplified urban visions at the same time. He is never formally associated with the modernist group, however.

Ponsen made the first of a number of trips to the Atlantic coast, historically a favorite location of American landscapists, in 1926. He travelled to Provincetown where he studied with Richard Miller and Charles Hawthorne at the latter's well-known studio.[21] *Gray Day at Provincetown* (cat. #10), one of a number of plein-air paintings characterized by the technique of painting in rapid, broken brushstrokes that Ponsen was to use extensively for the rest of his career, was painted during that summer.

As Ponsen began to develop as a landscapist, he continued to work on the figure, a subject which diminished in importance as his interest in the landscape expanded. Hawthorne was well-known for his character studies of fishermen, so it is not surprising that photographs belonging to Ponsen show the beach and the long pier that appear in *Gray Day* with the student artists assembled to work on studies from a figure posed on the beach (fig. 7). Ponsen's interest in Hawthornesque figure studies manifests itself in Muskegon, where he had copied the work of Gerrit Beneker in the Gallery before 1922, when one was displayed.[22]

The concept for, if not the direct inspiration of, the *Portrait of a Man in a Black Hat* (cat. #7) may be one of these outdoor sessions, in which the students had the opportunity to study the figure in the outdoor light. The *Man in a Black Hat* seems to be a study for the expanded *Seated Old Man with Cane* (cat. #8). Distinguished from the more formal portraiture of his conservative contemporaries by its simple wainscoted architectural background which stops at the sitter's waist thus silhouetting his upper body against the light background, he is linked to them by the retention of the clear three-dimensional quality, conventional color and detailed representation of facial features. Like Hawthorne and Beneker, who concentrated on fishermen, his is a sensitive study of a working-class person.

In subsequent years, Ponsen spent spring and/or summer months in a number of Atlantic coast destinations popular with American plein-air painters. In 1927, Ponsen spent the summer in Gloucester, Massachusetts; in spring, 1929, he painted in Boothbay Harbor, Maine (*Shipyard at Boothbay Harbor*, cat. #14; *Yacht Club Pier*, cat. #11; *An Old Pier* (fig. 8), *East Coast Boat Drydock*, cat. #15, was probably done at Boothbay Harbor); in 1938, he makes a return trip to Gloucester (*Gloucester Harbor*, cat. #17), and in 1939 he travels to the Gaspe Peninsula in Canada. He continues to produce popular and frequently exhibited landscapes in the Impressionist-derived style he develops in these early

Fig. 7 – Students painting, Provincetown, Massachusetts, 1926.

Fig. 8 – Tunis Ponsen. *An Old Pier*, c. 1929.

Fig. 9 – Tunis Ponsen. *Low Tide,* c. 1939

Fig. 10 – Tunis Ponsen. *An Overmantel: Decorative Painting,* 1928.

years. Ponsen exhibited work based on his trips to the Atlantic coast well after he ceased travelling to these sites. A painting inspired by the Gaspe Peninsula trip of 1939 called *Low Tide* (fig. 9), for example, was exhibited beginning in the early 1940s, at least twice in the 1950s and again in the retrospective exhibition at the Hackley in 1967.[23]

George Oberteuffer helped Ponsen obtain a fellowship and teaching assistant's position in the Graduate Atelier of the School of the Art Institute for the academic year 1927-28. In the Spring, Ponsen's *An Overmantel: Decorative Painting* (fig. 10), done as part of a competition, won the Bryan Lathrop Travelling Fellowship, providing Ponsen with $800 that had to be immediately applied to foreign travel. The painting, as it appears in newspaper reproductions from the period, suggests the work of Arthur Davies in its representations of weightless, dreamy figures arranged in a pattern in the landscape. Ponsen, like many artists in America, yearned for the opportunity offered by the scholarship. Chicago artists as varied as Francis Chapin, Archibald Motley, Jr. and Anthony Angarola made study trips to Europe in the late 1920s, each of them seeking and learning different things from the experience.

Unlike the others, though, Ponsen's trip was a return to his happy memories of childhood – family, friends, a familiar language and landscape. Other immigrant artists who settled in Chicago, like Emil Armin or William S. Schwartz, left Europe to escape persecution. Although Ponsen sought the same opportunities as they did in America, his life in the Netherlands was pleasant and he left friends and family behind. Judging from the work he brought back, most of Ponsen's six months abroad were spent in Holland, exploring the area around Delft, (*Windmill near Delft,* cat. #19) as well as returning to his native Wageningen where he painted numerous scenes including *Backyards of My Childhood* (cat. #18), a view from the creek that ran behind his childhood home. The Dutch landscapes depict a countryside of peace and fertility, devoid of nostalgia or romance. Ponsen's fascination with the windmill, a potent symbol of the fecundity and prosperity of the Netherlands, is seen in the numerous paintings he made of this subject. A commercially produced series of images of 25 different windmill designs that he brought back from this trip is further evidence of his interest in this subject. Several distinct types appear in paintings that were successfully exhibited well into the 1930s.[24] *Windmill near Delft* depicts a distinctly different type of windmill than that in *Windmill* (fig. 11). In the latter, the windmill and a distant church spire appear to tower over the landscape and people below, foreshadowing the compositions of his urban landscapes of the 1930s.

Ponsen travelled to Belgium and France as well as the Netherlands, but of the 40 paintings he declared when he returned to the United States in 1929, 36 were Dutch scenes. The remaining four were Parisian scenes. *Barges on the Seine* (cat. #21), *Morning on the Seine* (cat. #22) and *A Street in Paris* (cat. #20) were based on sketches done in Paris, if not actually completed on his trip. The fourth Parisian scene, *Fishing on the Seine* (fig. 12 is the small version of the painting done in Paris on which the prize-winning painting was based) won the Martin Cahn prize at the American Annual at the Art Institute of Chicago in 1929 as well as the Dixon prize at the South Side Art Association Spring Exhibition of the same year. One is reminded of the Parisian paintings of Ponsen's countryman, J. B. Jongkind, when looking at *Barges on the Seine*. In both Ponsen's painting and Jongkind's *View of Notre Dame* (1864, fig. 13), the industrial life of the city is pictured along the strong diagonal of the Seine River. As in *Fishing on the Seine*, the Cathedral of Notre Dame is silhouetted against the horizon. The use of the strong diagonal of the river as an organizing principle echoes the composition of *Windmill near Delft* as well as the earlier *Gray Day at Provincetown*. At the same time one is reminded of the Chicago river scenes which Ponsen begins to paint in the early 1930s. In both the Parisian and Chicago scenes the waterway is the psychological focus of the painting, and the broad, flat, undetailed color areas that are characteristic of paintings like *Chicago Silhouettes* (cat. #25) appear for the first time in pictures like *Barges on the Seine*.

The European paintings foreshadow Ponsen's most modern and most emotionally resonant paintings in other ways as well. In his most compelling work, like

Fig. 11 – Tunis Ponsen. *Windmill*, c. 1928.

Fig. 12 – Tunis Ponsen. *Fishing on the Seine*, c. 1928.

Fig. 13 – J.B. Jongkind. *View of Notre Dame, Paris*, 1864.

Fig. 14 – Jean Crawford Adams. *View from the Auditorium.*

Fig. 15 – Belle Baranceanu. *Factory by the River,* c. 1930.

Fig. 16 – Richard Chase. *The City at Night,* ca. 1930.

Chicago Silhouettes, Chicago River Industrial Scene (cat. #25) and *Chicago River Scene* (cat. #26), he chooses points of view that reveal something beyond "objective" vision. Like the view in *Backyards of My Childhood*, Ponsen chooses an unusual vantage point. Rather than painting the most characteristic aspect of the scene, as Ponsen often did in his popular seascapes, he shows the viewer the "back side" of the houses in Holland and the skyscrapers in Chicago.

Ponsen's urban vision, while sharing some of the qualities of other Chicagoans who painted the city, is unique. The large, flat, simplified forms of the identifiable skyscrapers towering over the small buildings along the Chicago River reveal his interest both in the commercial and industrial base of the city and the vocabulary of modernism. This connects him with such Chicagoans as Jean Crawford Adams (*View from the Auditorium*, fig. 14) and Belle Baranceanu (*The Factory by the River*, fig 15). While Ponsen's paintings share the Precisionist esthetic of Crawford, Raymond Shiva (*Chicago, MCMXXIV*, fig. 3) or Raymond Jonson (*The Night, Chicago,* fig. 1), he never constructs an unpopulated urban vision. We always see the faceless, universal working class figures, fishermen, or leisure strollers. He distinguishes himself from the conservative artists with whom he often exhibited, like Richard Chase, whose dramatic view of the Chicago skyline, *The City at Night* (fig. 16), verges on illustration. Perhaps closest to Todros Geller's *Michigan Avenue Bridge* (fig. 17), whose towering architecture dwarfs the tiny figures peering over the bridge railing, Ponsen's vision is one that is deeply connected to the human realm despite is glorification of the man-made wonders of the modern city. In that sense, his work combines, like so many other Chicagoans, the urban realism of the Ashcan School of the early 20th century with the modernist vision of the Cubist-inspired Precisionists to create a uniquely midwestern image of the city.

Chicago's technological modernity was celebrated in the Century of Progress International Exposition of 1933-34. Ponsen not only was invited to display his work in the exhibition of paintings and sculpture[25] and the exhibition of prints held at the Art Institute in conjunction with the fair, he was inspired to do a series of paintings of the grounds. The futuristic buildings and sleek, machine-inspired design that dominated the fair inspired a number of Chicago artists. In *World's Fair, Chicago* (fig. 18), Jean Crawford Adams emphasizes the curves of the bandshell and verticals of the flagpoles to create a nearly abstract image conveying the wonders of modern technology. Emil Armin's *The Fair and Fishing* (fig. 19) shares Ponsen's viewpoint and a more representational quality, but his brilliant color and purposeful primitivizing makes the landscape vibrate with energy. Ponsen's vision of the fair (*Chicago World's Fair*, cat. #27) relies on conventional representation of space, but shares the modern interest in the life of the city represented in brilliant patches of flat color. Never averse to commercial activity, Ponsen consigned several of his paintings of the fair, *Southern Entrance* and *Illumination*, to Groh and Company to sell. References to paintings titled *The Fair – Gray Day* and *Ramp and Rain*, both exhibited during and after the fair, indicate Ponsen's high level of interest in the subject.[26]

By the early 1930s, Ponsen had cast his lot with the conservatives, exhibiting with the Chicago Galleries Association and the South Side Art Association. However, the fluidity of the Chicago art community enabled Ponsen to be among the exhibitors at several shows at Increase Robinson's Studio Gallery, one of the few commercial venues for modernists in the early 1930s and to participate in the most egalitarian art event of the period – the open-air art fair in Grant Park in 1932. According to a newspaper account, "bills to the amount of $250 were thrust into the astonished hands of Tunis Ponsen at the Grant Park Art Fair" by "a stranger [who] admired Ponsen's watercolors and said he'd take the whole lot." The article describing Ponsen's success in selling his entire stock of paintings on the first day of the fair is subtitled "Bohemian Scene Draws Many Visitors Despite Cloudy Skies," conveying the public perception of the fair as one dominated by radicals. In fact, the fair attracted a wide range of artists, many feeling the effects of the Depression. Described by the young artist Gertrude Abercrombie as a site of diversity and community, a place where she "met all kinds of people, classes, colors, creeds, everything...and everybody loved each other,"[27] the fair in Chicago attracted artists of all persuasions.

Fig. 17 – Todros Geller. *Michigan Avenue Bridge*, 1930.

Fig. 18 – Jean Crawford Adams. *World's Fair, Chicago*, c. 1933

Fig. 19 – Emil Armin. *The Fair and Fishing*, c. 1934.

The Chicago paintings, all done in the 1930s, are also clearly allied with the Regionalism that was sweeping the entire country during the Depression era. Ponsen was employed on the government sponsored art programs, although it is not clear how long or how actively. We know one of his works (*Winter Scene*) was acquired by Libertyville High School from the Public Works of Art Project (PWAP), the shortest-lived and earliest of the government art programs.[28] Ponsen's name also appears on the rolls of artists working on the easel project of the Illinois Art Project (IAP) of the Works Progress Administration (WPA) which spanned the years 1935-43.[29] Because Ponsen's self-sufficient nature probably balked at this kind of help from the government, his participation may have been limited. Even though he was enjoying some success as an artist during this period, this program may have been a welcome source of income in needier moments. Letters from a friend in the late 1930s reflect some concern with finances and problems selling paintings; this was undoubtedly alleviated by the mid 1940s.[30]

The isolationist mentality of this period combined with the enormous amount of government supported art mandating painting of the American Scene – images of American life, often idealized and stereotypical – encouraged the production of images of small town or rural life that embodied the traditional ideals of America. In an effort to distinguish themselves from Europeans, American artists during this period self-consciously sought to make representational images with no reference to the abstraction or intellectual modernism of Europe. Artists in Chicago, both conservative and modernist, were perfectly positioned to take up the ideals of this period. Most of them already worked primarily in representational styles and the kinds of subjects that were most popular were those that emerged out of the Midwest – farms, small towns in the heartland, local industrial activity, and the positive potential of the typical American city.

Ponsen's urban scenes, with their emphasis on the redemptive possibilities of the modern metropolis, fit the mandate. So do the scenes of small towns and midwestern farms he begins to paint during this period. Ponsen had always travelled to the southwestern

Michigan farm of his sister and her husband, Arnolda (Nolda) and Herman Schogt, for weekends, holidays and vacations. The never-married Ponsen considered them, along with their daughter Angenita, born in 1918, his family, and maintained very close relations with them all of his life. Their farm and nearby sites provided him with subject matter almost all of his mature artistic career. Because he never learned to drive an automobile and was limited to the bus and train for transportation, his geographical circle was circumscribed. After his visits to the Atlantic coast in the late 1930s, he never went further than his Chicago neighborhood, the scenic towns of Illinois or the rich agricultural settings of southern and western Michigan for inspiration.

Ponsen's images of fertile Michigan farmland resemble the Regionalist landscapes popularized by Grant Wood, John Steuart Curry and Thomas Hart Benton. The panoramic *Midwest Landscape with Storm* (cat. #32) has the large, flattened color areas characteristic of Ponsen's work during this period. Although a cluster of farm buildings appears among the gently rolling hills, the painting puts emphasis on the cycles of nature, the coming storm and the ultimate fertility of the land. During this period of economic deprivation, drought and farm failures, artists in the United States chose to represent rural America as a fecund and rich reservoir ready to yield up its bounty. Like Curry's *Wisconsin Landscape* (fig. 5) or Chicagoan Elizabeth Colwell's *A Kentucky Road* (location unknown)[31], the landscape is panoramic, peaceful, cultivated and fertile.

Later landscapes like *Apple Tree* (cat. #37), reminiscent of the work of Vincent Van Gogh, focus on a single landscape element and rely more on broken, visible brushstrokes and the brilliant, pure color characteristic of mature Impressionism. *An Old Tree* (cat. #38), done in acrylic paint and dating to his latest period, demonstrates the continuity of interests throughout his career.

His paintings of small towns in the Midwest – *Country Train Station* (cat. #30), *Galena, Illinois* (cat. #28), *Midwest Backyards* (cat. #29) – have analogues in the work of local artist William Schwartz (*Untitled [City*

Street], fig. 20) and Aaron Bohrod (*Waiting for the 3:30*, fig. 21), who similarly extol the virtues of small-town America in their work. Compared to the composition of Schwartz, with its stylized, flattened planes, Ponsen's paintings appear traditional, yet his *Train Station* closely resembles Bohrod's work of about the same time. Along with the more conventional urban representations of his home on Oakenwald Avenue (*House on Oakenwald*, cat. #35), which Ponsen painted numerous times, emphasizing the quiet and tranquil small-town quality of the neighborhood, Ponsen's contribution to regionalism in Chicago is clear.

In *Galena, Illinois* and *Midwest Backyards*, Ponsen's view from the quiet intimacy of the backyard rather than the public and active main street is parallel to the view in *Backyards of My Childhood* and *Chicago Silhouettes*. In each case, Ponsen takes the opportunity to represent the aspect of the scene that is less often represented, but far more revealing. The resonance and quiet mystery of the images in which we see the "hidden" side of a scene make them some of his most interesting works.

In works like *Chicago Fishing Scene* (cat. #32), which may correspond to works with titles like *City's Edge* or *South Chicago Shoreline* mentioned in newspaper accounts and exhibition records, Ponsen combines his interest in the picturesque boating and fishing scenes of the East Coast with the regional interests he developed in the 1930s. It is similar in color to *Gloucester Harbor* (cat. #17) and shares its high viewpoint, diagonal shoreline and a horizon defined by vegetation. The scene that Ponsen paints resembles the quaint harbors of the Massachusetts and Maine coasts much more than that of Lake Michigan, where the water and sky merge at the horizon, the opposite shore never visible.

A group of images painted from his studio window span his entire career, beginning with *The Repair Gang* done in the late 1920s, to *Rainy Day* (cat. #33) and *Burning Cigarette* (cat. #34) of the late 1930s and even the undated *Snow in Chicago Alley* (cat. #36). In these works, Ponsen positions the viewer outside the main activity of the event, separate and detached. The idiosyncratic point of view that Ponsen repeats throughout his career may be related to his own shyness and self-protectiveness, if not isolation.

Fig. 20 – William Schwartz. *Untitled (City Street)*, c. 1938.

Fig. 21 – Aaron Bohrod. *Waiting for the 3:30*, c. 1941.

Ponsen's public popularity reached its peak in the late 1930s. Of the 14 times he participated in juried exhibitions at the Art Institute, only one was after 1938.[32] In that year, he was invited to have a one-person exhibition at the Drake Hotel under the sponsorship of the All Illinois Society of the Fine Arts. Although the 47 paintings exhibited included few, if any, Dutch scenes from the trip a decade earlier, a number of images inspired by his travels to the East Coast from the same period were shown. Inclusion of a number of urban scenes like *Chicago Silhouettes*, chosen as the cover illustration for the brochure, indicates Ponsen's pride in these works. Many of the images have titles that have associations to weather conditions (*After the Storm*, *Hills in Sunlight*, *Belated Snow*) or seasons (*Autumn*, *Midsummer*), underscoring his continuing interest in the atmospheric conditions that affect light and color.

In the postwar period, the taste for representational art was supplanted by the rise of Abstract Expressionism. Even in Chicago, artists like the members of the "Monster Roster" were coming to grips with developments in New York.[33] Ponsen himself attempted abstraction (*Sunbeams through the Clouds*, cat. #49; *Abstract*, cat. #50). Other Chicagoans like Don Baum and Gertrude Abercrombie were producing work linked to Surrealism while continuing the tradition established by Ivan Albright. Even as he experimented with abstraction, Ponsen continued to paint representational landscapes and cityscapes (*Heavy Snow*, cat. #39) similar to his earlier work.

Like his Hyde Park neighbor Abercrombie, he responded to the urban renewal that began in Hyde Park in the 1950s (fig. 22). Ponsen's painting of the skeleton of half-destroyed buildings surrounded by a multi-colored fence of old doors (*Demolition in Hyde Park*, cat. #40) contrasts markedly with Abercrombie's *Doors* (fig. 23). Abercrombie's doors dominate the painting, isolated from their original construction site, resonating mysteriously, acting as a device that cuts off the space and communicates her own internal struggles with isolation and loneliness.[34] Painted with precise clarity, there is no conventional attempt to create a sense of space and atmosphere, certainly no fixing of weather or time of day. Abercrombie is interested

Fig. 22 – Demolition site in Hyde Park, 1957.

Fig. 23 – Gertrude Abercrombie. *Doors (3-Demolition)*, 1957.

solely in internal life – this is the closest to an urban landscape that she ever paints – and was certainly inspired to paint the doors because of their personal emblematic significance as devices of separation. Abercrombie had also spent the happiest time of her life in a building that was destroyed by urban renewal, giving additional personal weight to the subject. Ponsen's image has his usual skillful objectivity; although not illustrational, it is a record of this important and pervasive activity.

The most interesting work of his later period include several still life paintings and a group of arrangements of objects in his studio that form an integrated whole. The *Arrangement on a Marble Counter* (cat. #41), *The Japanese Vase* (cat. #43) and *Still Life with Sansevieria* (cat. #44) are probably the earlier works. In the *Arrangement on a Marble Counter*, Ponsen incorporates personal allusions, in the form of earlier paintings, *Angenita with Doll* (cat. #42) and the study for *Barges on the Seine* (cat. #21). The very loosely rendered image of the artist's beloved niece linked with a reference to his European trip are combined with a group of still life objects – bottles, fruit, books – that do not have personal associations.

The Japanese Vase and *Still Life* both include books open to reproductions of works by artists Ponsen presumably admired, including Van Gogh and Cézanne. While the influence of Van Gogh is reflected in some of his work (see *Apple Tree*, cat. #37), Cézanne's work does not seem to have had a direct effect. Ponsen certainly was familiar with the post-impressionists, already well represented in the Art Institute collection; he also attended exhibitions of modern European art.[35] A measure of the limited influence of the more modernist artists on his work is seen in these skillful and interesting, but conventional, still lifes.

The second group of arrangements, brilliantly colored views of his home-studio, are probably ten to twenty years later and evidence Ponsen's more successful late formal experiments. *Red Drop Leaf Table with Bottles* (cat. #45), *Room with Red Drop Leaf Table* (cat. #46), and *An Open Door* (cat. #47) show us more about Ponsen's life than any of the more guarded and conventional still lifes of an earlier period. Showing the viewer his present working space with examples of his own work from various periods on the walls, they serve as a summation of his artistic activity. We see his simple furnishings: his chest of drawers through an open door; the brilliant red drop leaf table with the remains of a meal. The slight spatial distortions, the dazzling color, and the material simplicity bring to mind Van Gogh's *Bedroom at Arles*, a mainstay of the Birch Bartlett Collection donated to the Art Institute of Chicago in 1926.

Ponsen had an active artistic life, during which he exhibited with a number of predominantly conservative artists' organizations like the South Side Art Association, the Chicago Galleries Association, the All Illinois Society of the Fine Arts and a number of other artists' exhibition groups on a regular basis. He was selected regularly for the juried Annuals at the Art Institute of Chicago, certainly the most prestigious venue for any Chicago artist. He was also a member of the oldest artists' organization in town, the Chicago Society of Artists, a group that bridged the gap between modernists and conservatives.[36] He was invited to become a member of the Renaissance Society, an exhibition group that counted among its members artists who took a wide variety of approaches. He held classes in his studio most of his life, taught on a part-time basis at the Chicago Academy of Fine Arts and in the last decades of his life, taught very successful classes at several community arts centers.[37]

His personal life is a bit more elusive. He lived outside the major artists' enclaves for most of his life, in the neighborhood just north of the artist-heavy Hyde Park and far from the other major concentration of artists on the near north side of the city. By the time he moved to the house on Harper Avenue in 1952, the artist's colony on nearby 57th Street, active since the period immediately following the end of the World's Columbian Exposition of 1893, was only a decade away from destruction.[38]

Ponsen never had his own family, and if he had any long-term relationships of a romantic nature after the 1920s, they were kept quite secret. He was very close to his sister, brother-in-law and niece, admitting in a rare written display of emotion to depression at the death of his sister. In a letter of June 9, 1967 to Mrs. Berg in Muskegon, Ponsen responds to her sympathy note of several months earlier: "Since my sister passed away, I seem to have lost interest in things...I have to try to get out of this depressive mood."[39] When he moved into the large house on Harper Avenue, he rented rooms to students, establishing a surrogate family; when a student moved on, he would often give him or her a painting.[40]

According to his niece, he always travelled with friends. He had a close relationship with Ethel Crouch Brown, another Hyde Park painter whose family summered in western Michigan and with whom he often painted there.[41] His address book included the names of artists as diverse as Emil Armin, Ruth van Sickle Ford, Richard Chase, Gus Dalstrom, and Beatrice Levy, attesting to his status in both the traditional and modernist art worlds. He left little in the way of personal information – no journals, diaries, and few personal letters survive. What does survive indicates that Ponsen was a decent, kind human being, earning his popularity with his amateur students through an always respectful critique of their work.[42]

Ponsen's last decade included two solo exhibitions– the first, at the Chicago Public Library in 1961 and the final one, in 1967, at the Hackley Gallery. His skill as an artist and lack of rigidity allowed him to bridge the gap between traditional and modern, although on balance his work came down firmly in the former camp. He led a life free of drama, firm in the belief that what he saw was more important than what he felt. What we do know about Ponsen helps us to understand the distance he places between himself and some of his subjects and the idiosyncratic viewpoint he establishes for others. While these devices allow Ponsen to remain objective and unassuming, the viewer is given a window into the feelings of an artist who prided himself on painting what he saw.

– S.W.

NOTES

[1] Hirschl and Adler Galleries, *The Paintings, Drawings and Lithographs of William S. Schwartz* with essay by Douglas Dreishpoon (New York: Hirschl and Adler Galleries, Inc., 1984); Maureen A. McKenna, *Emil Armin: 1883-1971* (Springfield: Illinois State Museum, 1980; Maureen McKenna, *Julia Thecla: 1896-1973* (Springfield, Illinois: Illinois State Museum, c. 1985); Susan Weininger, *Gertrude Abercrombie and Friends* (Springfield, Illinois: Illinois State Museum, 1983); Kent Smith and Susan Weininger, *Gertrude Abercrombie* (Springfield, Illinois: Illinois State Museum, 1994); Mandeville Gallery, *Belle Baranceanu – A Retrospective* with essays by Bram Dijkstra and Anne Weaver (La Jolla, California: University of California, San Diego, 1985); ACA Galleries, *Anthony Angarola: An American Modernist* with essay by Matthew Baigell (New York: ACA Galleries, 1988); Betty Rymer Gallery, *A Tribute to Kathleen Blackshear* with essay by Carole Tormollan (Chicago: School of the Art Institute of Chicago, 1990); Wendy Greenhouse and Susan Weininger, *A Rediscovered Regionalist: Herman Menzel* (Chicago: Chicago Historical Society, 1994); Illinois State Museum, *John Warner Norton* with essays by Jim L. Zimmer and Richard N. Murray (Springfield, Illinois: Illinois State Museum, 1993); Jontyle Theresa Robinson and Wendy Greenhouse, *The Art of Archibald J. Motley, Jr.* (Chicago: Chicago Historical Society, 1991); . Dawson and Jonson have received more extensive treatment in print. For Dawson see especially Mary Mathews Gedo, *Manierre Dawson (1887-1969): A Retrospective Exhibition of Painting* (Chicago: Museum of Contemporary Art, 1976); for Jonson's early years in Chicago see especially Ed Garman, *The Art of Raymond Jonson, Painter* (Albuquerque: University of New Mexico Press, 1976), Elizabeth Ann McCauley, intro., *Raymond Jonson: The Early Years* (Albuquerque: Art Museum, University of New Mexico, 1980). In addition to these catalogs, extensive information about Chicago artists is found in Esther Sparks, *A Biographical Dictionary of Painters and Sculptors in Illinois, 1808-1945* (Ph.D. dissertation, Northwestern University, 1971) which includes an entry on Ponsen.

[2] J. Z. Jacobson, *Art of Today: Chicago, 1933* (Chicago: L. M. Stein, 1932). Published on the eve of the Century of Progress, the World's Fair that was a celebration of technology and modernity, Jacobson's book was an attempt to boost the mostly unappreciated modern Chicago artists who worked in the city.

[3] Aside from a very few exhibition catalogs, the major publications dealing with this group are those of William Gerdts, *Art Across America: Two Centuries of Regional Painting 1710-1920* (New York: Abbeville Press, 1990) and *American Impressionism* (New York: Abbeville Press, 1984).

[4] There is one early reference commercial work among Ponsen's papers. A letter dated 2 October 1926 from Gibson Catlett of Gibson Catlett's Studio informs Ponsen that because of diminished business he will no longer be employed doing real estate exhibits. He does praise Ponsen's work and promise him a bonus, however. Ponsen was a graduate student at the School of the Art Institute, judging from the fact that he is listed in the closing ceremony brochure in spring, 1927 as having won several honorable mentions. Taking on commercial work would have been logical considering his almost certainly difficult financial circumstances. This information is among Ponsen's papers. The Tunis Ponsen papers belong to Angenita Morris, Ponsen's niece, who generously made them available for the research on this essay, hereinafter referred to as the Ponsen papers. Most of my information on Ponsen was dependent on this material and the extensive chronology compiled by Pat Coffey, who graciously shared it with me well in advance of my writing of this essay.

[5] Newspaper clipping from the *Christian Science Monitor*, 26 May 1932, Ponsen papers.

[6] The Previewer, "Portraits on Exhibition in New Gallery Show," undated clipping, Ponsen papers.

[7] See the undated clipping in the Ponsen papers which discusses *The Repair Gang* of ca. 1930. The unidentified author of the article says of Ponsen, "Frankly he protests that he builds only as he sees, regardless of theories."

[8] For the modernists in Chicago, see Susan Weininger, "Modernism and Chicago Art: 1910-1940," in Sue Ann Prince, ed. *The Old Guard and the Avant-Garde* (Chicago: University of Chicago Press, 1990, 59-75.

[9] Jacobson, *Art of Today*, pp. xvii-xviii.

[10] Ponsen kept a signed photograph of Falise and a pamphlet of World War I cartoons by Raemakers among his belongings, attesting to their importance to him. They are in the Ponsen papers.

[11] This information comes primarily from handwritten notes, probably for a lecture that Ponsen delivered on the occasion of the 1967 retrospective exhibition of his work at the Hackley Gallery. It varies a little bit in its chronology from that in the 1931 brochure for Ponsen's exhibition there in which his first classes with Kensler are dated to 1921. It is possible that he sketched with Kensler before formally enrolling in classes.

[12] See the reviews of his exhibitions by Lulu Miller in the Muskegon press in his scrapbook, Ponsen papers. A typed list of works in the 1922 exhibition is in the Ponsen papers. Of the 26 works exhibited, nine are marked sold. Many portraits were done on commission and belonged to the sitters. The *Portrait of Al Boelkins* (1929), a Muskegon native, formerly in the collection of the Muskegon Museum of Art may be a reflection of some of these early portraits. A portrait of Boelkins (perhaps preliminary to the 1929 version), an old friend who also worked as a paperhanger and decorator, was exhibited in Ponsen's 1923 Hackley show. A newspaper obituary of 17 November 1958 from *The Muskegon Chronicle* is in the Ponsen papers.

[13] For the School of the Art Institute of Chicago, see Charlotte Moser, "'In the Highest Efficiency': Art Training at the School of the Art Institute of Chicago," in Prince, ed., *Old Guard*, 193-208.

[14] Buehr, in addition, painted figural impressionist scenes. See Gerdts, *Art Across America* 2:316.

[15] Betts lived from 1873-1961. See Sparks, *Biographical Dictionary* 1:280 and Union League Club, *American Art in the Union League Club of Chicago: A Centennial Exhibition* with essay by Esther Sparks (Chicago: Union League Club, 1980), 8-9.

[16] Ponsen's work is almost all undated. I have used a variety of methods to place his work chronologically. Sometimes there are references to the works in exhibition records or newspaper articles. Variations in titles and the fact that Ponsen often did several versions of one image creates a subset of problems with this method. At best, it yields a general terminus for the composition because many of the paintings seem to have been exhibited over a period of years and were not necessarily done immediately before the exhibition. The only reference I have come across that relates specifically to the *Arrangement with Eggs,* for example, is in a review by Edith Weigle of the South Side Art Association Summer Show of 1941 in which she describes Ponsen's prize winning painting as a "Still life with onions, sprouts, eggs in an overturned bowl and pitcher." While this seems to be the same painting, 1941 seems to be too late a date for its creation based on its style (there are other references to still life paintings by Ponsen in exhibition reviews but without a reproduction or description there is no way of associating this evidence with a specific painting). Ponsen travelled to a variety of places to paint and the pictures relating to those locales can sometimes be dated to the time of the particular trip. For example, he painted in Provincetown in the summer of 1926, so the paintings with Provincetown subjects would generally be dated accordingly. However, Ponsen often did watercolor sketches that he developed into oil paintings in his studio after his return home. In fact, this became his standard practice fairly early in his career. So it is not at all certain that the paintings Ponsen exhibited with titles referring to European or East Coast trips were actually done *in situ,* immediately upon returning or even several years later. A general sense of development of both style and attitude toward subject matter emerges from a study of the works which can be dated with certainty, and I have used this as a framework for placing the works for which there is no external or internal clue to date of production; other evidence could easily emerge which would alter my dating.

[17] School of the Art Institute of Chicago, Graduation Program, 1924, Ponsen papers.

[18] Ponsen won Class Honorable Mention for Figure and Head painting in 1927, School of the Art Institute Closing Exercises, Ponsen papers.

[19] Nancy Hale and Fredson Bowers, *Leon Kroll: A Spoken Memoir* (Charlottesville: University Press of Virginia, 1983), 59.

[20] Hale and Bowers, *Kroll,* 59.

[21] For Hawthorne see Gerdts, *Art Across America*, 1:55-56 and Union League Club, *Centennial Exhibition*, 15.

[22] For Beneker, see Gerdts, *Art across America*, 1:57, where Beneker is referred to as "the most directly indebted to his teacher [Hawthorne]."

[23] Taking into consideration the difficulties in connecting particular works with exhibition records, as well as Ponsen's practice of working from watercolor sketches in his studio – theoretically enabling him to use the sketches he made on the spot as the basis for paintings made years later – the exhibition history of *Low Tide*, based on existing evidence, is as follows: Association of Chicago Painters and Sculptors, Chicago Galleries Association, 1941, #42; South Side Art Association (Windermere Hotel), 1945; South Side Art Association (Mandel Brothers), n.d.; Renaissance Society Members Show, ca. early 1950s; All Illinois Society of the Fine Arts, ca. 1954; Hackley Museum of Art, 1967.

[24] *The Village Windmill,* for example, was exhibited in the Michigan Artists show at the Detroit Institute of Arts in 1934 (#260); it is reproduced as one of the items of interest in the exhibition in the *Detroit Free Press,* December 1933, Ponsen papers.

[25] Ponsen's painting, *Rock Quarry,* was exhibited. It is listed in the catalog, *A Century of Progress Exhibition of Paintings and Sculpture* (Chicago: Art Institute of Chicago, 1933), 74, #618. According to the catalog, the painting measured 19-3/4" x 23-3/4" so it cannot be the large *Stone Quarry* (cat. #24) in the present exhibition. It may, however, be a smaller version of this work.

[26] Records of the consignment and the references to exhibits including Ponsen's Century of Progress paintings are in the Ponsen papers. The popularity of the subject among Chicago artists is attested to by the exhibitions devoted to the subject. For example, Ponsen was involved in an exhibition sponsored by the Lighting

Institute at their Gallery which included 25 paintings by eight artists of night scenes of the fair and an exhibition of eight artists at the Antique Galleries of Marshall Field's (Department Store).

[27] Smith and Weininger, *Abercrombie*, 14; this quote is from a taped interview Abercrombie made with Studs Terkel in 1977.

[28] A brochure in the Ponsen papers refers to an exhibit featuring *Winter Scene*, along with other works of art acquired by the School from the PWAP, on May 23, 1935. The PWAP had officially ended on June 30, 1934.

[29] Public Works of Art Project, *Report of the Assistant Secretary of the Treasury to Federal Emergency Relief Administrator* (Washington, D.C.: United States Government Printing Office, 1934) includes Ponsen on p. 69, listing his address as 1031 East 45th Street, Chicago. He is also listed on the easel painting project of the IAP, although misspelled as Tunis Posen, in George J. Mavigliano and Richard A. Lawson, *The Federal Art Project in Illinois 1935-43* (Carbondale and Edwardsville: Southern Illinois University Press, 1990), 130. For the art projects in Illinois, see also Maureen McKenna, *After the Great Crash: New Deal Art in Illinois* (Springfield: Illinois State Museum, 1983).

[30] A letter of 1 February 1940 from Frances Cordes to Ponsen states that she is sorry "that you have not been faring well from your painting," Ponsen papers.

[31] This painting is reproduced in Jacobson, *Art of Today*, 56.

[32] In 1949, he exhibited *Storm Clouds in Spring* in the Chicago and Vicinity Show (no. 200). He also exhibits for the last time at the Michigan Artists Exhibition at the Detroit Institute of Arts in 1937, where he had exhibited regularly since 1927.

[33] For postwar developments in Chicago art see Franz Schulze, *Fantastic Images* (Chicago: Follett Publishing Company, 1972).

[34] For Abercrombie, see Weininger, *Gertrude Abercrombie and Friends*, Smith and Weininger, *Gertrude Abercrombie* and Rockford College Art Gallery, *The 'New Woman' in Chicago* with essay and biographies by Susan Weininger (Rockford, Illinois: Rockford College Art Gallery, 1993).

[35] Exhibition catalogs among his papers indicate he attended exhibitions of European modernists early in his career. For example, he kept copies of a catalog of an exhibition of American modernists called *4 Painters: Albers, Dreier, Drewes, Kelpe* at the Arts Club of Chicago in 1937 and a 1931 catalog from the Chester Johnson Gallery of a *Special Exhibition of Paintings, Drawings, and Watercolors*, all by European modernists.

[36] For the Chicago Society of Artists, see Louise Dunn Yochim. *Role and Impact: The Chicago Society of Artists* (Chicago: Chicago Society of Artists, 1979).

[37] He taught at the Blue Island Art Club and the Flossmoor Art Club, south suburban amateur groups which also had regular exhibitions. References in the Ponsen papers.

[38] The 57th Street art colony was headquartered in buildings built for the World's Columbian Exposition. These structures were destroyed to make way for urban renewal in 1962. See "Art Colony Plays Swan Song," *Hyde Park Herald*, 9 May 1962.

[39] Carbon copy of letter to Mrs. Berg, in which he also discusses plans for the upcoming retrospective exhibition at the Hackley Gallery, dated 9 June 1967, Ponsen papers.

[40] Taped interview with Angenita Morris made by Pat Coffey, October 1992.

[41] Morris-Coffey interview, October 1992.

[42] In letters to Mrs. Berg (9 June 1967) and Mrs. Russell Damm (5 November 1967) of Muskegon, he makes a special point of kindly praising their work, Ponsen papers.

Significant Events in the Life and Career of Tunis Ponsen (1891-1968)

BY PATRICK COFFEY

VICE PRESIDENT MARKETING

CITIZENS INSURANCE COMPANY OF AMERICA

Compiled from the artist's personal memorabilia, original exhibition catalogs, contemporary newspaper accounts and countless hours of pleasant conversation with the artist's niece, Angenita Schogt Morris.

I. THE NETHERLANDS YEARS: 1891 - 1913
(Artist's Age - birth to 22)

Tunis Ponsen's niece, Angenita Schogt Morris, remembers well her mother Arnolda's stories about the Ponsen family life in Wageningen, the Netherlands. Angenita Van Brakel was a young widow with two small children when she met and married a local house painter, Johannes Ponsen. Arnolda is the first born of this second marriage in 1889, followed by Tunis in 1891 and another daughter, Ger, in 1893. In later life, Arnolda and Tunis look back on their childhood years as a time of great happiness. One can picture young Tunis helping his father with his house painting trade. (Later, it will put him in good stead upon his emigration to America.)

A surviving small painting (fig. 24) indicates that the adolescent Tunis is already exhibiting considerable natural talent. The painting is inscribed on the reverse, "Painted by Tunis Ponsen, age 14. Copied from a painting in the Ryjks Museum."

Life for the Ponsen children is forever changed by the unexpected deaths of their father in 1907 and mother in 1909. The older children are working and keep the family together in the family home for as long as they can. In 1911, Tunis receives his first formal training in the arts when he begins a period of study in drawing with the sculptor, August Falise, and the landscape artist, Louis Raemaekers. (Raemaekers acquires a worldwide prominence later when he becomes the leading political cartoonist of World War I.) This study culminates in 1912 when Tunis is awarded a certificate of his ability to teach drawing at the elementary school level.

During this same period, Tunis and his childhood sweetheart, Cato Van Boekering, fall in love and engage to marry. With the European economy in shambles and war looming on the horizon, the young couple agrees that Tunis will go to America. When he has earned enough money, he will send for Cato. On April 13, 1913, twenty-two year old Tunis Ponsen arrives at Ellis Island, New York, aboard the steamship Potsdam.

II. THE MUSKEGON YEARS: 1914-1923
(Artist's Age 23-32)

1914-1916

By 1914, Tunis has settled in Muskegon, Michigan, where he earns a living as a housepainter and decorator. Later that same year, his sister, Arnolda, also emigrates from the Netherlands with her new husband, Herman J. Schogt (pronounced "Scott"). Herman had emigrated from the Netherlands two years earlier, first to Chicago and then to Benton Harbor, Michigan, where he purchased a small fruit orchard on Pipestone Road. Through sheer coincidence, Tunis and his sister find themselves in close proximity to each other as part of a large number of Dutch immigrants who choose to settle in Southwestern Michigan.

When Tunis has saved enough money, he arranges passage to America for his fiancée, Cato. However, during the long, hazardous voyage to America, Cato meets and falls in love with another young man in a whirlwind shipboard romance. When Tunis meets the ship in New York, he is devastated by the news that Cato is marrying someone else! As Tunis never marries, one can speculate that there is a connection between this one great failed romance and the love he will develop in his painting for the melancholy and the grey, sunless day.

Tunis' sister, Arnolda, and her husband, Herman Schogt, are the artist's only family in America during his lifetime. The bond between them is constantly nourished by frequent visits. Until Arnolda's death a half-century later, Tunis is a regular live-in guest in the Schogt family home for major holidays and summer vacation periods. As Tunis never learns to drive an automobile, he relies on bus and train for the trip to Benton Harbor from Muskegon and, later, from Chicago.

Fig. 24 – Painting by Tunis Ponsen, age 14.

Fig. 25 – Tunis Ponsen enlists in American army

Fig. 26 – Tunis and Angenita

Fig. 27 – Tunis Ponsen. Business card.

1917

Tunis has not forgotten his interest in the arts. With the money he has saved, he travels to Chicago where he spends six months studying drawing at the School of the Art Institute of Chicago. On his return to Muskegon, he decides to apply for U.S. citizenship. In a preliminary application, he describes himself as "…color white, complexion fair, height 6 feet 1 inch, weight 155, color of hair light, eyes blue, other visible distinctive marks none." He speaks with a definite Dutch accent, but not one which is difficult to understand. He lists his address as 628 Sanford Street, Muskegon.

1918

Tunis enlists in the American army and serves for the duration of the war. (fig. 25) That same year, Arnolda Ponsen Schogt gives birth to her first and only child, a daughter whom she names Angenita in memory of her own deceased mother. Tunis is completely captivated by little Angenita who becomes the joy of his life. (She fondly remembers Tunis as her "third parent.") His affection for his little niece is evident in a charming photo showing the beaming artist hoisting Angenita on his shoulders (fig. 26).

1919

While his interest in fine arts has persisted, Tunis is faced with the problem of supporting himself. A surviving business card (fig. 27) announces the firm of Teuling & Ponsen, painters, decorators and paperhangers who "…also have a Fine Selection of Wall Paper." The address of the firm is Muskegon Heights, Michigan.

1921

For the first time, Tunis exhibits two oil studies in a show for local amateur artists held at the Hackley Art Gallery (now known as the Muskegon Museum of Art). That September he enrolls in the gallery's evening study classes under the instruction of local artist, Wilbur C. Kensler. Gallery director, Lulu F. Miller, is taken with Tunis' talent and promises him that when he has developed his skills to the point where it is merited, she will arrange an exhibition of his works at the Hackley Art Gallery.

1922

In December, Tunis' work has developed to the point that Lulu Miller delivers on her earlier promise and arranges a one-person exhibition of his work at the Hackley Art Gallery. In reviewing the exhibition for the *Muskegon Chronicle*, she writes,

> There has been placed on view this week in the north gallery a collection of small sketches in oil which on three counts should claim the attention of Muskegon people. First from the artistic point of view they have merit. Technical faults there are in plenty, but these are more than compensated for by a sincerity and a genuine feeling and an artist's grasp of his subject. Second, these sketches are all bits of familiar scenes about Muskegon - the sand dunes at Lake Michigan park, with glimpses of the lake - groups of boat houses, a dock, the bridge at Ruddiman's creek, the paper mills seen from North Muskegon, a bit of the colony at the base of Pigeon Hill along Muskegon Lake, all seen with an artist's eye keen for the picturesque in the most commonplace subject. Last, and by no means least, the artist himself is of Muskegon, a young man, Tunis Ponsen by name, who has made his home here since coming to this country eight years ago. There are about thirty sketches in the collection and they are for sale at prices that seem absurd considering their quality. It would seem that there must be many people in Muskegon who will gladly make the exchange of a few dollars for a picture that in the years to come, if the present promise of the artist reaches fulfillment, may be worth much more than was paid for it, and in any case such encouragement can only be a source of satisfaction to those who give it.

1923

A year of studying and painting passes. In December, Lulu Miller arranges the second one-person exhibition of Tunis Ponsen paintings at the Hackley Art Gallery. She writes again in her review for the *Muskegon Chronicle*,

> …This week there were placed on view in the west gallery, twenty-four of Mr. Ponsen's paintings representing work done in the past year, and the strides he has made in these twelve months are apparent to those who have watched with interest his efforts…The technical faults in the pictures are due to inexperience, and time and study will remedy them. Their genuine artistic qualities will be recognized by any artist.

III. THE SCHOOL OF THE ART INSTITUTE OF CHICAGO: 1924-1926
(Artist's Age 33-35)

1924

In January, Tunis enters the School of the Art Institute of Chicago in a full-time degree program. Because of his age, prior training and experience, he is given advanced standing. His instructors include Karl Buehr, George Oberteuffer and Leon Kroll.

1925

Tunis completes the usual three-year study program in just 18 months. In June, he graduates from the School of the Art Institute of Chicago. His graduation photo (fig. 28) will be the only studio portrait of his lifetime. Later in the year, the Hackley Art Gallery holds its third one-person exhibition of Tunis Ponsen's work.

1926

With his basic studies completed, Tunis continues in the graduate program at the Art Institute of Chicago (AIC). He spends the summer studying with Charles Hawthorne and Richard Miller at the Provincetown Art Colony (Massachusetts). Tunis later gives one of his personal favorites to his sister, Arnolda (cat. #10, *A Gray Day At Provincetown*). Upon his return to Chicago with a large number of canvases, Tunis establishes an apartment studio at 4422 Oakenwald in Chicago and becomes an active member of the South Side Art Association. He paints one of the Oakenwald buildings many times (cat. #35, *House on Oakenwald*).

Fig. 28 – Tunis Ponsen. School of the Art Institute of Chicago graduation portrait, 1925.

Fig. 29 – Tunis Ponsen. Watercolor study for catalogue #39.

Fig. 30 – Tunis Ponsen. Watercolor study for catalogue #22.

IV. THE MUSEUM EXHIBITION YEARS: 1927-1939

(Artist's Age 36-48)

1927

A pivotal and breakthrough year in Tunis' career to date. In May, the Hackley Art Gallery holds another one-person exhibition of 33 Tunis Ponsen paintings, including 16 from the Provincetown group. The *Muskegon Chronicle* review of the exhibition begins,

> *Muskegon is having a rare experience, an exhibition of paintings of a product of its own gallery. For the balance of May there is hung in Hackley Art Gallery the works of a young native of the Netherlands who came to Muskegon a few years ago, and less than six years ago was a student in the gallery evening classes here.*
>
> *Since that time, the advancement of Tunis Ponsen has been rapid, and today he is winning recognition. Muskegon will have the right to take pride in his career in the future only in the measure that it gives him recognition now. Too many communities are known to history only for their failure to recognize the genius in their midst.*

Tunis spends the summer of 1927 painting with friends at Gloucester, Massachusetts (cat. #16, *Wharfs At Gloucester*). Upon his return to Chicago, George Oberteuffer arranges for him to receive a tuition scholarship in the Graduate Atelier of the School of the AIC. In addition to his own study, he serves as an instructor in the undergraduate program. In October, Tunis is honored when one of his Gloucester paintings, *Near the Harbor,* is selected for the juried 40th annual Exhibition of American Paintings and Sculpture at the Art Institute of Chicago. For the first time, at the age of 36, Tunis Ponsen is awarded a place alongside America's finest living artists. The *Muskegon Chronicle* reports the event as follows,

> *Friends of Mr. Tunis Ponsen in Muskegon will be interested to know that his painting, 'Near the Harbor', done at Gloucester during the past season, has a place in the 40th exhibition by American painters which opened at the Chicago Art Institute Thursday of this week. This*

distinction lifts the artist from the amateur class,
as the exhibition is second only to the International
Show at the Carnegie Institute.

This year also marks the first of eight appearances of one or more Ponsen works in the juried Michigan Artist's Exhibition held annually at the Detroit Institute of Arts (DIA).

Finally, 1927 marks his first use of the watercolor medium. Tunis discovers during the summer of 1926 at Provincetown what a difficulty it is to transport large numbers of painted canvases back to Chicago. For the trip to Gloucester, Tunis solves his logistical problem by using watercolor as the medium for his preliminary sketches and studies. Later, back in Chicago, some are used as the basis for studio paintings. Often a 20" x 24" painting first, followed by a 24" x 30" or larger version of his favorites. This use of watercolor becomes a consistent pattern for the balance of the artist's career (figs. 29 and 30).

1928

In May, Tunis is awarded the Bryant Lathrop Traveling Scholarship as the outstanding artist in the Graduate Atelier of the School of the AIC. The *Muskegon Chronicle* reports the event,

Mr. Tunis Ponsen whose rapid advancement in the field of painting has been watched with interest by many persons in this city, has just been awarded the Bryant Lathrop Scholarship prize, carrying with it the sum of $800.00 which according to the terms of the award, is to be used in foreign travel. With three other recent prize winners, Mr. Ponsen expects to leave early in June for Paris. The honor conferred upon Mr. Ponsen enables him to realize a dream long cherished.

Tunis departs in June and returns to his native Netherlands where he spends the summer painting scenes of his childhood. After a stay in Paris, he returns to Chicago with 40 canvases, four Parisian scenes and the rest Dutch.

Upon his return, he is honored by the selection of five of the prior summer's Gloucester paintings for inclusion in the juried 32nd Anniversary Exhibition of Artists of Chicago at the AIC.

In addition to this success in Chicago, Tunis has two works (*Waterfront, Provincetown* and *Low Tide, Gloucester*) accepted for the annual Michigan Artist's Exhibition at the DIA. The Illinois Academy of Fine Arts December exhibition held at the Illinois Women's Athletic Club includes *The Twins, Gloucester*. Finally, the Hackley Art Gallery once again includes Ponsen in its annual exhibition.

1929

In May, the Southside Art Association holds its annual Spring exhibition at the Stevens Hotel near downtown Chicago. The *Chicago Herald & Examiner* carries a photo of a Ponsen painting with the caption,

PRIZE WINNER-This painting, 'Fishing on the Seine', by Tunis Ponsen, is one of the prize winners at the exhibition of the Southside Art Association, now in progress at the Stevens Hotel. Miss Berdie Colbert is inspecting the canvas.

The painting is a larger studio version of one of the Parisian compositions from the previous summer.

On October 23, *Chicago Herald & Examiner* art critic, Francis Farmer, selects Tunis' works to serve as the focal point for his review of the year's major exhibition. He writes,

Aglow with color and replete with daring adventures in the realm of composition, the forty-second annual exhibition of American Painting and Sculpture is formally to be opened at the Art Institute tomorrow afternoon. Tunis Ponsen entitles an especially alluring canvas 'Fishing on the Seine'. A strong Ponsen portrait of a great American actress, Catherine [sic] Cornell, exhibits both the strength and the self-centered intensity of its subject, and, in her gown of glowing red, some luscious color and very remarkable fabric painting (cat. #9).

Tunis Ponsen is awarded the Martin B. Cahn Prize by the exhibition jury for *Fishing on the Seine*, the best painting by a Chicago artist.

1930

The year begins with an exhibit of Tunis' work at the Bryn Mawr Woman's Club in Chicago.

During the spring, Tunis travels to Boothbay Harbor, Maine, where he completes his third series of New England coastal and harbor scenes. At the AIC, one of these paintings, *Yacht Club Pier* (cat. #11) is included in the 34th annual exhibit of Artists of Chicago. (This painting will later be acquired by the Hackley Art Gallery.) *An Old Wharf* and *Little White Cottage* are selected for the juried Chicago Society of Artists annual exhibition.

Tunis is one of three artists selected for a major exhibition held in October at the Chicago Galleries Association, 220 North Michigan Avenue. The exhibition is a smashing success for him and is covered by the major Chicago newspapers.

Writing in the October 5 Sunday edition of the *Chicago Herald & Examiner*, art critic Irwin St. John Tucker says,

> Another artist exhibiting at the Chicago Galleries this month, Tunis Ponsen, has the architectural conception; but he takes for his subjects trees, barns and windmills. Perhaps the best - certainly the most appealing to me - of the powerful canvases here is that of the old trees surrounding a red roofed barn. They convey a sense of guardianship; there is a comradely feeling in the way their leafy roofs protect the top and their running interlaced shadows frame the bottom of the flimsy old structure.
>
> Mr. Ponsen is a Hollander by birth and painted many of these scenes in Holland. He brings to his art the serious solidity of a Dutch conception. He builds his foundations deep and true, and on them erects his painting - even though it be of a subject as transitory as a cloud or a sail flapping in the wind- with careful methodical structure, until the passing moment he has seized upon stands fixed for all time.
>
> This man takes what we used to call modernism, gets the good out of it, and makes it glorious.

The *Chicago Tribune* of Sunday, October 12, uses a large photo of a Ponsen painting captioned,

> *'Fishing on the Seine', by Tunis Ponsen, who is one of three artists showing in the current exhibit at the Chicago Galleries Association. Mr. Ponsen was born in Holland and among his paintings are many of Dutch subject. Others are of French origin, but the majority are American, with Boothbay Harbor, Maine, of first importance. The painting reproduced won the Martin B. Cahn prize last winter at the Chicago Art Institute.*

The *Chicago Evening Post* prints an even larger photo of a Ponsen painting captioned, "A Shipyard, Boothby Harbor, Maine - Tunis Ponsen. In an exhibition of Ponsen's paintings at the Chicago Galleries Association October 1 to 22."

The *Chicago Herald & Examiner* uses a photo of a third Ponsen painting bearing the caption, "Village Mill" - Tunis Ponsen. In Ponsen's one-man show at the Chicago Galleries Association."

This three-person exhibition belongs to Tunis Ponsen!

The jury for the 43rd annual national Exhibition of American Painters and Sculptors at the Art Institute selects two Ponsen paintings, *The Repair Gang* and *Derricks on the Chicago River*. This is the third time Tunis is selected for this national juried exhibition. A neighborhood South Side newspaper reports the event,

> Of particular interest to Oaklanders at the current American show at the Art Institute is a painting of a local scene by Tunis Ponsen of 4422 Oakenwald Avenue. This picture is called 'Repair Gang' and was painted by Mr. Ponsen from his upstairs window at 44th and Oakenwald.

(Two paintings hanging in this same exhibition are of special interest. They are #43, *The Tornado* by John Steuart Curry which will later be acquired by the Hackley Gallery in Muskegon and #207, *American Gothic* by Tunis' contemporary, Grant Wood.)

In December, the Chicago Galleries Association holds a general exhibition of the artist members. The two Ponsen paintings included are *Yacht Club Pier* and *Reflections*. During 1930, Tunis also exhibits at the DIA and the Hackley Art Gallery, Muskegon. At the age of 39, Tunis Ponsen seems to be on his way to national recognition.

1931

Tunis selects *An Old Pier* (fig. 8), another of the Boothbay Harbor paintings, as his entry in the annual juried Michigan Artists Exhibition organized by the DIA. When the same exhibit travels to the Flint Institute of Arts (Flint, Michigan), the general public is invited to cast their votes for their favorite painting. The winning painting will be purchased by the Flint Institute of Arts as the first painting for the permanent collection. *An Old Pier* is the public choice.

The *Flint Journal* reports the event,

> *Purchase of one of the paintings showing at the Flint Institute of Arts in the Michigan Artists show was authorized at a meeting of the board of trustees yesterday. The picture is 'An Old Pier' by Tunis Ponsen, a young Michigan artist who is living in Chicago at present.*
>
> *The painting, which will be added to the permanent collection of the Flint Institute of Arts, is done in a strong, rich technique, and while definitely in the modern style, is worthy of appreciation based on academic standards. It represents old shacks and a pier along the shore of a bay. There is a bright blue sky and clouds - all of which are in glowing colors. This will be the first painting to take a place in the institute's permanent collection.*

The March one-person exhibit held at the Hackley Art Gallery in Muskegon is reviewed in the *Muskegon Chronicle.*

> *Tunis Ponsen depicts scenes of peaceful repose, lovely bits along the Massachusettes and Maine shores, sincerely interpreted and pleasing to the eye. Gloucester Harbor, Mass., and Boothbay Harbor on the Maine coast have furnished material for a group of Ponsen paintings in the present exhibition. Wharves and shipping seem to have a special fascination for the artist whose fishing boats riding at anchor look easily capable of sailing away to the fishing grounds and the day's haul…Two strong portrait studies appear in the Ponsen collection and there are three still life studies, notably a Japanese vase in harmonious settings, and a group of realistic vegetables.*

At the AIC, three Ponsen canvases are selected for the 35th annual Artists of Chicago exhibit, *A Filipino, City's Edge* and *Castles of Today.* The Pennsylvania Academy of Fine Arts includes *Canal Bridge in Delft* in its annual American artists exhibition. Rounding out the year, Tunis also exhibits in two Chicago Galleries Association exhibitions, an Illinois Academy of Fine Arts exhibition held at the Art Gallery of the Illinois State Museum in Springfield and in an exhibition of flower painting at the Studio Gallery, Chicago.

1932

In March, Tunis is one of nine artists featured in an exhibition at the Chicago Galleries Association. *Chicago Tribune* art critic, Eleanor Jewett, writes,

> *From Jessie Arms Botke, we turn to Tunis Ponsen who has made strides recently in his painting. He offers a very fine portrait, a few still life arrangements and various out of door scenes. His painting is rich in feeling and atmosphere and in quality.*

In his review of the same show, Tom Vickerman writes in the *Chicago Evening Post,*

> *Of all the contributers to the painting shows of the Chicago Galleries Association, probably no deserving artist has been more taken for granted than Irma Rene Koen….There is probably no one on the Galleries' membership list, always excepting Tunis Ponsen, who can surpass her.*

On Thursday, May 26, Tunis receives what will be the only national recognition of his entire career. The prominent national newspaper, *The Christian Science Monitor,* publishes a large photo of a Ponsen painting. The caption reads, *Barges on the Seine:* (cat. #21) From a Painting by Tunis Ponsen (Courtesy of the Art Institute of Chicago to the *Christian Science Monitor*)." The accompanying article reads,

> *When Mr. Ponsen was asked what he had to say about his picture – whether he had any definite theories to expound or any special message which he wished his interviewer to pass on to the public – he smiled a little shyly and said: 'None. You know, I just paint the thing I see the way I feel it. I have no particular theories. I just try to paint well.'*

Fig. 31 – Tunis Ponsen painting at the farm in 1947.

There seems, indeed, to be no explanation at all beyond the simple fact that Mr. Ponsen, with two artist friends, went one day down the reaches of the Seine from the center of Paris, in search of interesting subject matter. Presently he found himself engrossed in these barges which lay idle in a half-sunny, half-gray light. But Mr. Ponsen admits that perhaps the prevailing grayness of his native Holland creeps unawares into some of his paintings of other countries.

Mr. Ponsen is one of the younger, but eminently successful of Chicago artists, having completed his art training in the graduate atelier of the Art Institute of Chicago and then, in the company of several other artists who had won traveling scholarships, gone to Europe for further inspiration and study. Among his contemporaries, his approach to painting stands out as conservative; yet he is up-to-date thoroughly in his ideas. This painting, for example, embodies his interest in portraying the third dimensional quality in nature. Notice how definitely the line movement leads directly into the canvas, so that one seems to be looking far below the surface of the Seine.

Mr. Ponsen's work has carried away important prizes and been shown in many exhibitions, where he is often classed most pleasingly as an 'artist's artist'.

In Benton Harbor, Arnolda and Herman Schogt purchase a 30-acre fruit farm with a small 19th century farmhouse, a chicken coup and three small producing orchards (apples, peaches and cherries). The farm is located on Napier Road some 10 miles outside of Benton Harbor. Angenita is now age 14. For the next 33 years, until Arnolda's death in 1966, Tunis will travel from Chicago by train and bus to spend holidays and a summer vacation with his only American family. The farm buildings and the rolling hills and orchards around this Michigan home become a favorite theme that he paints over and over again in each of the seasons. All of this work is done in watercolor which he finds much easier to transport to and from Chicago. Tunis works very sure and very quickly in the watercolor medium (fig. 31). Angenita remembers how she would leave the house in the morning and find on her return later in the day as many as a dozen watercolors spread out for her to see. Tunis always wanted to know which ones she liked best.

In Chicago, two paintings, *Boathouses* and *Stone Quarry* (cat. #23) are selected for the 36th annual Artists of Chicago exhibition at the AIC. Tunis also exhibits at the DIA and in an exhibition of self-portraits held at the Increase Robinson Galleries. Eleanor Jewett comments about Tunis' portrait when she writes in her Chicago Tribune review,

> *...Tunis Ponsen's self-portrait is not only an excellent likeless but also the story of the man inside, plodding, determined, forever ernest and honest.*

During this period, Tunis forms a close lifetime friendship with fellow Chicago artist, Ethel Crouch Brown. She had been one of his pupils at the School of the AIC when he served as a graduate instructor. Ethel and her husband and son also travel from Chicago to Michigan each year for a summer vacation in the greater Benton Harbor area. Tunis and Ethel paint together regularly.

1933

Early in the year, the AIC selects Tunis' new work, *The River*, for inclusion in the 37th annual Artists of Chicago exhibition. In May, the South Side Art Association holds its annual exhibition at the Hotel Sherman. Tunis is represented by three paintings, *Castles of Today*, *View from the Hill* and *Boothbay Harbor*.

But the exciting event of 1933 for all of Chicago is the Great Chicago World's Fair. After five years of planning, the Century of Progress Exhibition celebrating the 100th anniversary of Chicago's incorporation as a city is scheduled to open in June. A large new complex of buildings has been constructed to showcase Chicago to the world. The AIC is planning a major exhibition which will highlight the significant art movements of the past century along with the works of important contemporary artists worldwide. Artist's participation will be by invitation only.

The AIC has planned two separate exhibitions for the Chicago World's Fair which will run concurrently in two different wings of the museum from June 1

through November 1. Tunis is honored when his painting, *Rock Quarry*, is included in "A Century of Progress Exhibition of Paintings and Sculpture."

More surprising is the inclusion in "A Century of Progress Exhibition of Prints" of a Ponsen lithograph. Daniel Catton Rich of the museum staff has learned that Tunis is doing some experimenting with lithography. He is taken enough with the results to include *The Village Church* in the cataloged portion of the exhibition. (Three others, *Canal Bridge in Delft*, *Dutch Farmhouse* and *Old Farmhouse*, are included in an uncataloged selection of prints which are available to the public for purchase.) As the exhibition catalog lists the participating artists in alphabetical order, Tunis finds himself listed between Pablo Picasso and George Rouault.

During the year, Tunis is represented in a Chicago artists exhibition at the Increase Robinson Galleries by two works, *The Fair* and *Gray Day*. In December, the DIA includes *Village Windmill* and *Chicago Towers* in the annual Michigan Artists Exhibition.

1934

Like many others, Tunis is feeling the effects of the Great Depression. Artistic recognition has not brought with it the financial rewards needed for him to continue to devote full time to his own work. After seven years at the house on Oakenwald, Tunis needs more studio space so that he can supplement his income from the sale of his own works. A South Side newspaper reports,

> *Tunis Ponsen sends word that he has opened a studio at 1031 East 45th Street where he will conduct classes in drawing and painting on Tuesdays, Thursdays and Saturdays.*

Tunis will work in this studio for the next 16 years.

No less than eight exhibitions include works by Tunis Ponsen during 1934. At the AIC's 38th annual Artists of Chicago exhibit, he is represented by *After the Storm* and *Hill Village & Harbor*. The Toledo Museum of Art includes *Rock Quarry* in its 21st Annual Exhibition of Selected Paintings by Contemporary American Artists.

Hills in Michigan, Still Life and *Dutch Farmyard* are shown at the Chicago Society of Artists annual exhibition. The John P. Harding Galleries assembles a follow-up 2nd International Exhibition of Prints at the Century of Progress Graphic Arts Building which includes Tunis' lithograph, *House By the Bridge*. At the Orrington Hotel in Evanston, the University Guild of Evanston organizes an Exhibition of Paintings by Artists of Chicago. Tunis is represented by *Boat Houses.*

At the Chicago Galleries Association, Tunis is one of four featured artists. Eleanor Jewett covers the event for the *Chicago Tribune,*

> *The Chicago Galleries, 220 North Michigan Avenue, opened an exhibit of recent work by artist members yesterday. The artists concerned are Tunis Ponsen, Richard Chase, C. Curry Bohm and Arthur G. Rider.*
>
> *The little center gallery is hung with the paintings by Tunis Ponsen. These give a cheerful and colorful effect, although nothing of great importance emerges from the first impetuous glow the room arouses. However, the paintings fall into order after a second look and one comes out with a distinct recollection of the large interior, 'The Japanese Vase', a striking arrangement, the grays in 'South Chicago', the warm creams of 'Fishing on the Bridge', and the simple excellence of 'Portrait Sketch'.*

During 1934, Tunis paints what he will later come to regard as one of his finest works, *Chicago Silhouettes* (cat. #24). The year ends with the inclusion of *Hill Village & Harbor* in the annual Michigan Artists Exhibition at the DIA.

1935

This is a quiet year for Tunis. There are no museum exhibitions of his work. To help struggling artists financially during the Great Depression, the Public Works of Art Project purchases artworks which are then donated to various public institutions. In May, the Liberty Township High School holds an art exhibition. Group B consists of paintings and drawings acquired by the school from this project. #5 in Group B is titled *Winter Scene*, an oil painting by Tunis Ponsen.

At the Chicago Society of Artists November exhibition, Tunis is represented by *Wrecking the Old Mansion* and *The Approaching Storm.*

1936

In February, Tunis shows *Wrecking the Old Mansion* at the Chicago Galleries Association. The AIC includes *December Snow* in its annual Artists of Chicago exhibition. Tunis is once again represented in the DIA's Michigan Artists Exhibition.

1937

Winter Morning is selected for the 41st annual Artists of Chicago show at the AIC. The Chicago Galleries Association includes *Michigan Landscape* and the Chicago Society of Artists *Approaching Storm* in their annual exhibits. At the 12th annual fall exhibit of the All Illinois Society of the Fine Arts at the Stevens Hotel, Tunis is represented by *A Grain Elevator* and *The Abandoned Stone Quarry*. In December, Tunis exhibits in the annual Michigan Artists Exhibition at the DIA for the eighth and final time.

1938

In March, the All Illinois Society of the Fine Arts holds its third annual exhibit of watercolors. Tunis has been working more and more in the watercolor medium and submits *An Old Farm House* (the Benton Harbor farm) and *A Small Dutch Shipyard*. *Grant Park Harbor* is included in the 42nd annual Artists of Chicago exhibition at the AIC.

In May at the Drake Hotel, the All Illinois Society of the Fine Arts holds what will be the only major retrospective exhibition of Tunis Ponsen's lifetime. Tunis selects 40 paintings which span his career to date. *Chicago Silhouettes* is illustrated on the exhibition program cover.

Chicago Tribune art critic, Eleanor Jewett, covers the exhibition. The headline reads,

> *"Warm Colors Make News in Ponsen Exhibit," by Eleanor Jewett. The All-Illinois Society of Fine Arts is sponsoring a show of paintings by Tunis Ponsen at the Drake Hotel.*
>
> *Mr. Ponsen has long been one of our more intelligent and diligent painters. He has shown in many exhibitions and has received various honors. For a time one associated his name with canvases which were rather melancholy in character - rainy days seemed to have a fascination*

for him - and when he got a rainy day in conjunction with a nice wet expanse of tranquil lake, Mr. Ponsen was right in his element. There was nothing he could do about it but paint it, and then we had another moment of tranquil pathos to live through, even though our enthusiasm for his picture was real.

In the present exhibition this passion for grays is enlarged to a sincere liking of clear, warm colors and from a narrow stroke Mr. Ponsen has loosened his technique into a rolling, nonchalant freedom that lends itself admirably to the painting of landscape. The 'Rolling Hills' is probably the best illustration of this departure of the painter's talent.

Mr. Ponsen has a delightful sense of composition and of contrast. One of his most brilliant canvases is, 'A Rainy Day', where, from inside a warm, dry room replete with comfort (a state symbolized by an open book on the window-seat and a still smoking cigarette on an ashtray), one looks out upon a brisk April morning with young leaves on the trees and a fresh spring rain slanting down the street to the dismay of two young persons who are caught in it.

(Note: In her review, Ms. Jewett has confused *A Rainy Day* (cat. #33) with T*he Burning Cigarette* (cat #34).)

Another fascinating picture is the 'Still Life Arrangement', for which the artist's studio was plundered of many treasures. The detail in this is superb and the whole effect stunning.

Other than his regular trips to Michigan, Tunis has not traveled outside of the greater Chicago area since the 1929 trip to Boothbay Harbor, Maine. This summer he makes a return visit to Gloucester. *Gloucester Harbor* (cat. #17) results from this trip. In Gloucester, Tunis meets a young woman, Frances Cordes, with whom he will exchange letters for several years.

While Tunis is not yet aware of it, his years of regular exhibitions in major art museums are at an end. Works by Tunis Ponsen have been included in important museum exhibitions 34 times in the prior 17 years. There will be just two more during his lifetime. Those will occur 11 and 29 years into the future.

V. YEARS IN TRANSITION: 1939-1949
(Artist's Age 48-58)

1939

The year begins with a special January three-person exhibition at the Chicago Galleries Association. Paul T. Gilbert covers the event for the *Chicago Herald and Examiner*.

A triple show in one of Chicago's head-quarters of conservatism is drawing much favorable comment. Ruth Van Sickle Ford, Charles W. Dahlgren and Tunis Ponsen are having three one-man shows this month at the Chicago Galleries Association, 215 N. Michigan av.

…Tunis Ponsen is showing both landscapes and still lifes, and his views of the Gloucester area are particularly charming. In 'Harbor Scene' the boats rock quietly at the wharf, the water blue and serene. His work makes a refreshingly clean and harmonious impression.

At the spring exhibition of the South Side Art Association held at the Sibelius Club in April, Tunis is represented by *An Old Harbor*. That same month the Chicago Society of Artists celebrates its 50th anniversary with a major exhibition. Tunis' *Old Blacksmith Shop* and *The Abandoned Stone Quarry* are included. Eleanor Jewett writes in the *Chicago Tribune* under a headline which reads, "HITS WPA ART PROJECT FOR AID TO BAD PAINTING."

She writes,

…If you can overlook the WPA pseudo-art, there are several adequate paintings in the exhibit, paintings which would count as good art in any company. There are 'Old Blacksmith Shop' by Tunis Ponsen…

In June, Tunis receives a letter from one of his new friends from the Gloucester trip the year before, Frances Cordes. She writes, "I was sorry to hear that you are so discouraged with the financial results of your painting. I do hope the summer's work will mean success for you…"

The Great Depression has made life so difficult for Tunis that he resorts to removing finished paintings from their stretchers so that he can reuse them for new paintings. (Later, his estate will include dozens of these flat canvases, all of them the same size, 20" x 24".)

That summer, Tunis makes his fifth extended trip seeking new and fresh locations for his painting. This time he travels to the tip of the Gaspe Peninsula in Quebec Province, Canada. He returns with a large number of watercolors and small oil sketches on artist's board. These sketches and the larger versions which are painted back in Chicago are noticeably brighter than the New England paintings of the 1926 trip to Provincetown, the 1927 visit to Gloucester, the 1929 Boothbay Harbor paintings and, to a lesser extent, the prior summer's Gloucester paintings.

In Europe, World War II has begun.

1940

In February, Tunis hears again from Frances Cordes, who writes, "It certainly was a welcomed letter indeed, and I am very glad to hear from you. However, I am very sorry to know by it that you have not been faring well from your painting. I really can't blame you for not caring to write if things make you feel so low. I enjoyed watching you paint in Gloucester - on the hill that warm Sunday morning and by the docks at dusk. You did paint it so expressively that I know that it is not your painting that lacks personality, it is that things are not going well no matter what the trade."

Early in the year, the South Side Art Association opens its season. The *Chicago Tribune's* Eleanor Jewett reports,

The South Side Art association is entering its sixteenth year of exhibits and its first exhibit this season is in the club woman's bureau, Mandle Brothers. Five paintings are outstanding. The association is composed of artists and patrons.

'The Harbor' by Tunis Ponsen bears his familiar print. Mr. Ponsen has painted another of those gray days of which he is so fond and gives us boats and dock and the general air of placidity that his harbor scenes generally wear. It is an artist's picture and well handled.

During the summer, the Chicago Navy Pier Art Exhibit hosts the Fourth Annual Exhibition of Works by Chicago Artists. Tunis is represented by *Gaspe Shoreline* and *An Old House*.

The busy fall schedule finds Tunis participating in two important exhibits. At the Chicago Galleries Association, he is once again one of three artists selected for a special showing. Eleanor Jewett writes,

…Tunis Ponsen has an attractive group of landscapes to his credit in this same exhibition. He has one especially fine portrait of a young man, presented simply and naturally, but very well painted.

A landscape in grays is most intriguing. There are a few little summer landscapes that have feeling and atmosphere and on the whole one can write this group of pictures down to the credit side of a painter who has given us in earlier days many and many a worthwhile composition.

Mr. Ponsen is not a modernist, but he belongs to the modern school, leaning, if anything, toward an impressionistic type of suggestive work, brushing in his effects with a broad sweep and letting detail go as of small avail.

Late in the year, Eleanor Jewett again writes about Tunis under a column headline which reads, "TUNIS PONSEN IS MASTER OF WATER SCENES." She continues,

Various one-man exhibits of interest are scattered about town. In the Tudor gallery, Chicago Woman's Club, are paintings by Tunis Ponsen. Mr. Ponsen is well known for his delightful landscapes and more than delightful water scenes.

He paints a dock on a rainy day with a verisimilitude that sets you worrying about your lack of an umbrella. Just to hold one would give you greater courage to face that rhythmic drip.

The following week, Eleanor Jewett reviews the same exhibit in more detail under the column heading, "LIKES PONSEN'S EXHIBIT OF HARBOR SCENES". She writes,

One of the most distinguished of the month's exhibitions is that of landscapes and harbor scenes

by Tunis Ponsen at the Tudor gallery, Chicago Woman's Club. Mr. Ponsen is one of our well-known painters and his work is always a delight. These recent paintings were done on the Gaspe, that tongue of Canada which is still rich in primitive living, and at Gloucester.

'In Port' is a colorful little canvas showing a fishing boat drawn up beside the wharf. The shadows in the water are beautifully handled and the color and theme remind one of a Japanese print.

'Lifting Fog' is another striking picture, the grays as smooth and wet as fog itself. A group of tiny pictures is most intriguing and the larger paintings well repay a visit.

During the year, the 22-year-old Angenita marries H. Kenneth Morris. Ken becomes fast friends with Tunis who is a guest at their wedding.

1941

In February, Tunis celebrates his fiftieth birthday. In June, Edith Weigle reports in a Chicago newspaper,

The pleasant June days of the last week have seen the opening of several new exhibition. At the Windermere Hotel the members of the South Side Art Association are holding their summer show. More than 80 paintings are on view.

A number of prizes have been awarded…It was doubtless difficult for the judges to give the prizes in the still life compositions for there were so many submitted and a number were of almost equal excellence. Tunis Ponsen's first prize winner, called simply 'Still Life', proves again that the humblest objects may hold great beauty, for here are assembled onion sprouts, a few eggs in an overturned bowl, and a pitcher, all painted finely, delicately in subdued silvery tones. Ethel Crouch Brown's lively, vivid green 'Plants' was awarded second prize…

In October, Tunis is again one of three artists featured at the Chicago Galleries Association. Ernest Heitkamp reviews the show in a Chicago newspaper as follows,

Paintings by Marcena Barton, Tunis Ponsen and William Hollingsworth, Jr. are being shown by the Chicago Galleries Association for the next three weeks.

Here we have a diversified and balanced show-something for almost every taste. Marcena Barton shows cityscapes, landscapes and still lifes; Ponsen shows landscapes around Chicagoland, and Hollingsworth offers his sympathetic interpretations of the Southland.

The show also offers three different ways of painting. Take the two ways represented by Marcena Barton and Ponsen. They both paint things around Chicago, yet how different are their individual interpretations. You may prefer the tight manner of Marcena Barton; or, on the other hand, you may prefer the looser brushing of Tunis Ponsen. But stand away from these pictures and try to forget how they were done and judge only by the results. It's the picture that counts…

Another Chicago paper reports,

The Chicago Galleries Association opened an attractive exhibition yesterday which will continue to Oct. 27… Tunis Ponsen shares the gallery with Marcena Barton with a fine array of landscapes and scenes painted around Chicago. Mr. Ponsen came from Holland many years ago, but there is still more than a little of the Dutch in his psychology and where Miss Barton is apt to give us keen edges and a practical approach, Mr. Ponsen wraps every idea in his pictures with a wisp of mellow sentiment. One feels his heart behind his paintings while perhaps one is more cognizant of the brain behind Miss Barton's work.

Also in October, the Chicago Society of Artists holds an exhibition of the works of selected members at the Riverside Museum in New York City. The exhibition catalog foreward reads (in part), "…An exhibition of representative Chicago artists could never speak for any one school. Here now, as always, are the products of every culture, climate and background. Here again will proof be borne that the American scene is no more apposite to the Middle West than abstractionism is the clew to Paris. Five Ponsen works are included; three oils, *Boat Houses, An Old Blacksmith Shop* and *Old House, Lemont, Illinois,* and two watercolors, *Chicago River Scene* and *Still Life*.

December 7 - Pearl Harbor - the United States enters WWII.

1942

With all attention focused on the war effort, art exhibitions seem out of place and are few and far between. Tunis' only exhibition of the year is a one-person showing of 20 paintings at the Elm Place School in suburban Highland Park.

1943

In the Chicago Tribune edition of December 29, 1993, Rita Fitzpatrick writes about the wartime Chicago art scene,

'Chicago is the cultural center of America and the future art center of the world,' Dr. Dudley Crafts Watson, painter, author and lecturer at the Art Institute, told members of the Rotary Club of Chicago yesterday. Dr. Watson, along with twenty other well-known Chicago artists, was a special guest at the club's holiday luncheon at the Hotel Sherman.

'Dr. Watson introduced the guest artists, each of whom brought a prize painting to exhibit. Among them were Joseph Allworthy, Frances Badger, Charles Biesel, Marie Blanke, Ray Breinan, Ethel Crouch Brown, Edith Cassady, Richard A. Chase, Frank V. Dudley, Rowena Fry, Elmer Forsberg, Adolph Heinz, Rudolph Ingerle, Raymond Katz, Winifred Pleimling, Albin Polasek, Tunis Ponsen, Flora Scolfield and Ethel Spears.'

1945

Tunis joins the faculty of the Chicago Academy of Fine Arts where he will teach for more than twenty years. The Academy is second only to the School of the AIC as a source of professional instruction for serious students.

A *Joliet* (Illinois) *Herald News* story in April gives us the only surviving first-hand account of Tunis' painting technique. It reads,

With bold swift strokes, Tunis Ponsen made a vigorous and unusual still life come into being in a little more than an hour's work Sunday afternoon, when the Joliet Artist's League observed its April hospitality day.

Herbert Lemcke, program chairman, introduced Mr. Ponsen who, though he is not accustomed to demonstrating in public, belied his spoken timidity by painting just as though he were alone. He opened his demonstration with this remark, 'In a still life painting, you have to feel movement in the whole composition,' and he illustrated this with his basic charcoal sketch and again in the use of color.

In painting, Mr. Ponsen used long, straight strokes, much as he did in drawing. 'Straight lines are stronger than curved ones,' said the speaker. 'Even an apple must be drawn in straight structural lines first. This gives strength and depth.' He worked from the basic color to the lighter reflections and objected to too much superimposing because the clarity of color is then lost and a muddy effect results.

The active members of the Art League who were fortunate to see Mr. Ponsen's demonstration were amazed at the speed of his performance and looseless of his style: the bold long brush strokes, and the vigor and interest of the completed composition. Mr. Ponsen then did an abstraction of the same still life set up in pastels to illustrate interest in masses.

Eleanor Jewett mentions one of Tunis' newer works in the July 1, 1945, *Chicago Tribune* when she writes,

The artists of Chicago are well represented in two exhibitions that have been attracting attention. The Chicago No-Jury Society of Artists has a representative show in the Club Woman's bureau while the South Side Art Association has a large and varied group of pictures by professional members.

…We found the watercolors in the large room the most attractive things on view, tho an oil by Tunis Ponsen, 'Low Tide', won us completely in another room. Tunis Ponsen has struck a new

high in this Gaspe beachscape and its sparkle and vigor are sufficiently outstanding to make it a noteworthy contribution to any exhibition. It has charm, character, subtlety and beauty. It is a remarkable record of one of the most picturesque spots on the Canadian coast.

1947

The Chicago Society of Artists again holds an exhibition at the Riverside Museum in New York City. The catalog foreward reads (in part), "Chicago is a vast and cosmopolitan city; its artists are just as varied and as rich. They paint according to their tastes and interests, and they shall be judged solely by the quality of their work.

"The Chicago Society of Artists, again, as at our previous exhibitions at the Riverside Museum in 1939, 1941 and 1944, presents to New York what is, we feel, typical of the best art trends in present-day Chicago. Tunis is represented by two watercolors, *Heavy Snow* and *The Back Door*.

1949

Eleven years have elapsed since a painting by Tunis Ponsen has been exhibited at the AIC. As an honored alumnus of the School of the AIC, Tunis is invited to exhibit in a special showing of work by older alumni that will open one week after the 53rd Annual Exhibition of Artists of Chicago. Tunis accepts and is included in both shows. The 53rd annual exhibit includes Storm Clouds in Spring and the alumni show *Snow in an Alley* [sic] (cat. #36).

VI. PEACE AND PROSPERITY: 1950-1960
(Artist's Age 59 to 69)

1950

In January, Tunis is one of two artists featured in a two-person exhibit at The Chicago Galleries Association. *Tribune* art critic, Eleanor Jewett writes,

The Chicago Galleries Association has a superb January show of landscapes by John Bacus and landscapes and other subjects in oil by Tunis Ponsen. 'Snow Fences' and 'Tree Against Clouds'

are two outstanding canvases by Mr. Ponsen. Among the loveliest of the countrysides by John Bacus are 'Misty Morning' and 'Deep in the Ozarks'. This is a MUST exhibition.

Another Chicago paper reviews the same exhibition.

…Tunis Ponsen paints with a stronger brush than Bacus. His 'Tree Against Clouds' is wonderfully effective. The 'Snow Fence', a smaller canvas, is handled with skill and imagination. The whites are fascinating, pointed by the thread of color in the fences. 'My Old Coffee Pot' is outstanding among the several sturdy still lifes and 'Overpass' is a beautiful incident of bridge and boats. The exhibit by Mr. Ponsen is one of the finest that we remember in some time.

Writing in the *Chicago Daily News* of March 13, C. J. Bulliet comments about a Ponsen painting in an exhibition held at Mandle's by the Artists League of the Midwest. Bulliet writes,

Tunis Ponsen's winter scene is glamorous with snow, which, however, fails to destroy the ruggedness of the rural spot it covers. Ponsen, Hollander by birth, has something of the vitality of Van Gogh and Israels in his makeup.

1951

In February, Tunis is the subject of a one-person exhibition of recent watercolors. The *Chicago Tribune* headlines the event "STUNNING SHOW ON EXHIBITION IN WOMAN'S CLUB." Eleanor Jewett writes,

February has been remarkable for the number of attractive exhibitions in the galleries. A great many one-man shows added distinctly to the pleasure. The beautiful new gallery of the Chicago Woman's Club, 318 S. Michigan Ave., gave us an interesting group of water colors by Tunis Ponsen, a show which will run over into March. Mr. Ponsen has outdone himself in a number of the paintings, especially in the beautiful 'Old Tree'. It is one of the loveliest pictures of the year.

Mr. Ponsen also has been successful in a well handled winter landscape of snowy fields and with a charming fruit tree in full blossom. A row of willows bowing in the wind is a little suggestive of Van Gogh.

1952

Tunis has been enjoying a period of financial success. His own works have been selling steadily and he has been successful as a teacher, both in his own private studio and at the Chicago Academy of Fine Arts where he is now a regular instructor. With the money he has saved since the end of the war, he realizes a long-held dream and purchases his own home, the first he has ever owned. The house at 5809 Harper Avenue in Hyde Park (adjacent to Chicago) is a large, sprawling frame structure built in the 19th century. The house is located just a few blocks from the University of Chicago. It is so large that Tunis not only has plenty of room for his own living quarters and studio, but also several rooms which he is able to rent out to university students. Tunis now has enough extra room so that his Michigan relatives stay with him during their Chicago visits.

The Harper Avenue house has a regular flow of visitors. Some are pupils who come for private and group art lessons. Others are collectors who are interested in Tunis' work and want to own one of his paintings or watercolors. Neighbors report that it is a common sight to see someone leaving Tunis' home and walking down the street with a painting tucked under their arm. The remaining years are ones of peace and prosperity for the Dutch immigrant who almost forty years earlier came to America so that he and his childhood sweetheart, Cato Van Boekering, could live their lives together in the new land.

1953-1960

Tunis continues to participate regularly in the wide range of exhibitions that have become "standard" for successful artists of Chicago. These include the Chicago Galleries Association, the All-Illinois Society of the Fine Arts, the Renaissance Society, the Chicago Society of Artists and the Association of Chicago Painters and Sculptors. However, unlike past years when Tunis was more often than not the "star" of so many exhibitions,

he is now one of many included in the alphabetical lists of participating artists. He has become one of the old generation of Chicago artists, still highly respected but relegated to the past.

Some indication that Tunis still retains the same consistent high skill levels that have always distinguished his work is found in a *Chicago Tribune* review in April, 1955. Eleanor Jewett writes,

One of the finest events to occur in the current exhibitions about town is the awarding to Adam Emory Albright, veteran Chicago painter, of the All-Illinois Society of Fine Arts first prize for oils…Other excellent awards were made in this exhibit…The Margaret Dingle Memorial Award went to Tunis Ponsen for his fine stretch of shoreland, 'Fishermen's Homes'.

In 1956, the Illinois State Fair holds its tenth juried art exhibit of the work of professional artists in Springfield. This year, professional artists from seven midwestern states are invited to submit entries. Tunis is represented by an oil which he titles *My Studio Window*.

While still a regular instructor at the Chicago Academy of Fine Arts, Tunis has also become the teaching director of the Blue Island Art Club and the instructor of the Flossmoor Art Group, two local groups of amateur painters.

With the death of Adam Emory Albright in 1957, the 66-year-old Tunis Ponsen becomes the Grand Old Man of the Chicago art scene.

In May, 1958, Tunis is represented by an oil still life in the annual exhibition of works by artist members of The Renaissance Society at the University of Chicago.

VII. THE FINAL YEARS: 1961-1968
(Artist's Age 70 to 77)

1961

Two important exhibitions remain. In 1961, Tunis, now age 70 (fig. 32), is invited to assemble a group of paintings for a two-person exhibition at the downtown Chicago Public Library. The *Hyde Park Herald* of July 19 reports,

A critic once said, 'There is a kind of blunt Dutch honesty in a painting by Tunis Ponsen. He is never guilty of adding sugar and spice that might make a rich and popular pastry for rapid and eager comsumption. Rather, his work is as substantial and wholesome as bread - and no more difficult to digest.'

Just how well he spoke can be determined by visiting the Art Department of the Chicago Public Library. Ponsen is showing 13 paintings, beginning August 3 and continuing through the month.

A resident of Hyde Park, 5809 Harper Avenue, Tunis Ponsen's paintings reflect his community and his interests. Included in the library show are 'Demolition in Hyde Park' (cat. #40), 'Illinois Central Track', 'An Old Barn in the Dunes', 'Heavy Snow' (cat. #39), 'In Front of My Fireplace', 'Approaching Storm', 'Old Apple Tree' [sic] (cat. #37) and others.

The *Chicago Tribune* publishes its final review of a Tunis Ponsen exhibition on July 30. The review, which also includes a photo of *Heavy Snow*, reads,

> One of Chicago's older artists, and a young innovator will share the walls of the Art Room in the Public Library during August.

> Tunis Ponsen, for many years a member of the Chicago Society of Artists and the Rennaisance Society, was born in the Netherlands and studied under the Dutch sculptor, August Falise and the famous war cartoonist, Louis Raemakers. In Chicago, he continued his art studies under Karl Buehr, George Oberteuffer and Leon Kroll at the Art Institute and took part in many group shows in the 1920s and '30s. He has shown in other cities winning prizes and awards.

> Mr. Ponsen is a traditional painter of the impressionist school. His subjects are urban scenes and country landscapes. His palette is usually quiet and subdued; his work simple, solid, full of integrity. His followers feel an affection for his paintings, just as they do for those of his contemporary, the late Jeffrey Grant.

Fig. 32 – Tunis Ponsen, age 70.

Mr. Ponsen, who is now in his 70th year, says frankly that his work is of the conservative school. He has no prejudice against nonobjective painting, but feels that it should be judged on its own merits, and that traditional art should not be looked at from the nonobjective point of view. Both types of art have their place in our era, he feels.

1962

In May, the community of Hyde Park celebrates the centennial of its founding. Among other planned events is an exhibition of the work of the major artists who lived and painted in Hyde Park between 1890 and the present. The 45 artists selected include Carducius Plantagenet Ream, Karl Albert Buehr, Loredo Taft, Oliver Dennett Grover, Charles Frances Browne, Aaron Bohrod, Jessie Arms Botke and Tunis Ponsen. Tunis is represented by an oil, *Cherry Orchard, Benton Harbor.*

1967

There is one last hurrah for 76-year-old Tunis Ponsen. In June, he receives a letter from Mrs. Russell M. Damm inviting him to exhibit once more at the Hackley Art Gallery in Muskegon. It has been 36 years since his last exhibition there. Tunis responds,

Dear Mrs. Damm:

Your letter of June 5 certainly brought back many memories. I recall the pleasant times and the friendships of so many people connected with the Hackley Gallery, which goes way back (I hate to admit it) to World War I days and it is hard to believe that so many years have passed. It was during the time I painted the children of Mr. & Mrs. Harold Thurston, when I had an exhibit at the Hackley Gallery and "The Friends of Art" purchased my painting 'Yacht Club Pier, Boothbay Harbor, Maine.'

I recall vividly the pleasant association with the Thurstons, the Almys who was the director at that time. I still remember meeting the first director, Mr. Raymond Wyer, and, of course, the friendship and encouragement of Miss Lulu Miller, who became the gallery's second director, I always will cherish deeply.

Mr. Rinle Oldenburg, the custodian for many years, Mr. Wilbur Kensler, teacher and artist were wonderful friends to me.

But I better stop reminiscing. Now, in regard to giving a program and holding an exhibit, I have to admit that this will be a little difficult for me. I have given a few painting demonstrations for art groups but that was a few years ago. Giving a lecture will also be difficult for me.

Also I haven't a car which makes it perhaps a little more difficult. Now, would it be possible for you and some other members of "The Friends of Art" to come to Chicago and visit my studio and to see my latest paintings.

I have kept up painting all these years, besides teaching at the Chicago Academy of Fine Arts. I am still considered a conservative artist with a modern trend. I have tried some abstract painting, which, as you know, is very popular. So I would like to show my work to you before we would decide on a one-man exhibit.

Or perhaps the present director of the Hackley Gallery could also visit my studio to see my paintings. It is very easy to reach my studio by car as it is close to the University of Chicago.

I surely appreciate to have the opportunity, through your letter, to renew my connection with the "Friends of Art" and the Hackley Gallery. Hope to hear from you again. Thank you very much.

Most sincerely, Tunis Ponsen

While awaiting a response from Muskegon, Tunis gets what must have been a sad letter for him ending his 22-year association with the Chicago Academy of Fine Arts. Dated July 7, 1967, the letter reads,

Dear Mr. Ponsen:

It is with the utmost regret that I find we will be unable to renew your classes for the coming school year.

I am personally grateful to you for your devoted teaching of previous years, and hope, that in the future we may have you instruct at the Chicago Academy of Fine Arts again.

Sincerely, James Paulus, Dean

In Muskegon, the Friends of the Art at the Hackley Gallery persist and Tunis selects 12 paintings for what will be his final exhibition. They include *Chicago Silhouettes* (cat. #24), *Midwest Backyards* (cat. #29), *Gloucester Harbor* (cat. #17), *Morning On The River Seine* (cat. #22), and *A Rainy Day* (cat. 33). He travels to Muskegon for the November opening where he expresses his gratitude for his American beginnings a half-century earlier. (Four months later, the artist will be dead. How fitting it seems that the final exhibition of Tunis Ponsen's long career takes place at the Hackley Gallery, the same site of his very first exhibition 46 years earlier.)

1968

In January, Tunis slips on a patch of ice while walking to a nearby store and fractures his collarbone. He calls Angenita from the hospital to tell her what has happened. Angenita and her husband, Ken, travel to Chicago every weekend. While recuperating in the hospital, Tunis suffers a gallbladder attack which requires surgery. Peritonitis sets in and Tunis dies on March 9.

It is ironic that after so many lengthy reviews during his long, illustrious career as an important Chicago artist, The *Chicago Tribune* of March 11, 1968, requires just four sentences to report the death of this now obscure painter.

Services for Tunis Ponsen, 77, of 5809 Harper Avenue, will be held at 2 p.m. tomorrow in the chapel at 2121 W. 95th St. He died Saturday in Illinois Central Hospital. Mr. Ponsen was a landscape artist and taught at the Chicago Academy of Fine Arts since 1945. He leaves a niece.

– P.C.

MALE MODEL

1

REPOSING NUDE

2

YOUNG MAN WITH VIOLIN

3

STUDY OF A YOUNG GIRL

4

MAN HOLDING A BOTTLE, c. 1927

5

ARRANGEMENT WITH EGGS

6

PORTRAIT OF MAN IN BLACK HAT

7

SEATED OLD MAN WITH CANE

8

PORTRAIT OF KATHARINE CORNELL, c. 1929

9

GRAY DAY AT PROVINCETOWN, 1926

10

YACHT CLUB PIER, 1930

11

SELF PORTRAIT, 1928

12

SELF PORTRAIT WITH CIGAR, 1929

13

SHIPYARD AT BOOTHBAY HARBOR, MAINE,

c. 1930

14

EAST COAST BOAT DRYDOCK, c. 1930

15

WHARFS AT GLOUCESTER, c. 1927

16

GLOUCESTER HARBOR, c. 1938

17

BACKYARDS OF MY CHILDHOOD, c. 1928

18

WINDMILL NEAR DELFT, c. 1928

19

A STREET IN PARIS, c. 1928

20

BARGES ON THE SEINE, c. 1928

21

MORNING ON THE RIVER SEINE, c. 1928

22

STONE QUARRY, c. early 1930s

23

CHICAGO SILHOUETTES, c. 1934

24

CHICAGO RIVER INDUSTRIAL SCENE, c. 1930s

25

CHICAGO RIVER SCENE, c. 1930s

26

CHICAGO WORLD'S FAIR, c. 1933

27

GALENA, ILLINOIS, c. late 1930s

28

MIDWEST BACKYARDS, c. 1938

29

COUNTRY TRAIN STATION

30

MIDWEST LANDSCAPE WITH STORM

31

CHICAGO FISHING SCENE

32

RAINY DAY, before 1938

33

BURNING CIGARETTE, before 1938

34

HOUSE ON OAKENWALD

35

SNOW IN CHICAGO ALLEY, before 1949

36

APPLE TREE

37

AN OLD TREE

38

HEAVY SNOW

39

DEMOLITION IN HYDE PARK, c. late 1950s

40

ARRANGEMENT ON A MARBLE COUNTER

41

ANGENITA WITH DOLL

42

THE JAPANESE VASE, c. 1931

43

STILL LIFE WITH SANSEVIERIA

44

RED DROP LEAF WITH BOTTLES, c. 1950s

45

ROOM WITH RED DROP LEAF TABLE,
c. 1950s
46

AN OPEN DOOR, c. 1950s
47

VIEW OF CHICAGO THROUGH BIRCH TREES,
c. 1960

48

SUNBEAMS THROUGH THE CLOUDS, c. 1960s

49

ABSTRACT, c. 1960s

50

SELF PORTRAIT, 1964

51

All paintings on display in this exhibition are from the collection of Angenita J. Morris, unless otherwise noted.

1. **MALE MODEL**
   size: 38" x 30"
   unsigned
   oil on canvas

2. **REPOSING NUDE**
   size: 30" x 20"
   signed: lower right
   oil on canvas
   Collection of Muskegon Museum of Art
   Gift of Angenita J. Morris, Accession 80.60

3. **YOUNG MAN WITH VIOLIN**
   size: 38" x 31-1/2"
   signed: lower right
   oil on canvas

4. **STUDY OF A YOUNG WOMAN**
   size: 28" x 22"
   signed: lower left
   oil on canvas

5. **MAN HOLDING A BOTTLE, c. 1927**
   size: 32" x 26"
   signed: lower right
   oil on canvas

   Exhibited at Hackley Art Gallery (one-person exhibition), 1927; 32nd Annual Exhibition by Artists of Chicago and Vicinity, The Art Institute of Chicago, 1928, number 193.

6. **ARRANGEMENT WITH EGGS**
   size: 20" x 24"
   signed: lower right
   oil on canvas

   Exhibited in South Side Art Association Summer Show, 1941 (awarded first prize for still life).

7. **PORTRAIT OF MAN IN BLACK HAT**
   size: 24" x 20"
   signed: lower left
   oil on canvas

8. **SEATED OLD MAN WITH CANE**
   size: 40" x 34"
   signed: lower right
   oil on canvas

9. **PORTRAIT OF KATHARINE CORNELL, c. 1929**
   size: 36" x 30"
   signed: lower right
   oil on canvas

10. **A GRAY DAY AT PROVINCETOWN, 1926**
    size: 20" x 24"
    signed: lower right
    oil on panel

11. **YACHT CLUB PIER, 1930**
    size: 36" x 42"
    signed: lower left
    oil on canvas
    Collection of Muskegon Museum of Art
    Gift of Friends of Art, Accession 31.3

    Exhibited in the 34th Annual Exhibition by Artists of Chicago and Vicinity, The Art Institute of Chicago, 1930, number 158; 10th Semi-annual Chicago Galleries Association Members Exhibition, 1930, number 88; Hackley Museum of Art (one-person exhibition), 1931; Hackley Museum of Art (one-person exhibition), 1967; Hefner Galleries, 1985.

12. **SELF PORTRAIT, 1928**
    size: 36" x 30"
    signed: lower right
    oil on canvas

13. **SELF PORTRAIT WITH CIGAR, 1929**
    size: 42" x 36"
    signed: lower left
    oil on canvas
    Promised gift of Angenita J. Morris to the Muskegon Museum of Art

    Exhibited at Hefner Galleries, 1985.

14. **SHIPYARD AT BOOTHBAY HARBOR, MAINE, c. 1930**
size: 30" x 36"
signed: lower right
oil on canvas

Exhibited at Chicago Galleries Association, ca. 1930; Hackley Art Gallery (one-person exhibition), 1931.

15. **EAST COAST BOAT DRY DOCK, c.1930**
size: 26" x 30"
signed: lower left
oil on canvas

16. **WHARFS AT GLOUCESTER, c. 1927**
size: 20" x 24"
signed: lower right
oil on canvas

17. **GLOUCESTER HARBOR, c. 1938**
size: 25" x 30"
signed: lower right
oil on canvas

18. **BACKYARDS OF MY CHILDHOOD, c. 1928**
size: 24" x 30"
signed: lower left
oil on canvas

Exhibited at Hackley Art Gallery (one-person exhibition), 1967; Hefner Galleries, 1985.

19. **WINDMILL NEAR DELFT, c. 1928**
size: 26" x 30"
signed: lower right
oil on canvas

20. **A STREET IN PARIS, c. 1928**
size: 24" x 20"
signed: lower right
oil on canvas

21. **BARGES ON THE SEINE, c. 1928**
size: 30-1/2" x 26-1/4"
signed: lower right
oil on canvas

Exhibited in the 34th Annual Exhibition by Artists of Chicago and Vicinity, The Art Institute of Chicago, 1930, number 156; South Side Art Association 7th Annual Exhibition, 1930, number 83; Hackley Art Gallery (one-person exhibition), 1931.

22. **MORNING ON THE RIVER SEINE, c. 1928**
size: 24" x 20"
signed: lower right
oil on canvas

Exhibited in the South Side Art Association 7th Annual Exhibition, 1930, number 84; Hackley Art Gallery (one-person exhibition), 1931; Hackley Art Gallery (one-person exhibition), 1967.

23. **STONE QUARRY, c. early 1930s**
size: 30" x 36"
signed: lower right
oil on canvas

24. **CHICAGO SILHOUETTES, c. 1934**
size: 32" x 36"
signed: lower right
oil on canvas

Exhibited in a one-person exhibition at the Drake Hotel, sponsored by the All-Illinois Society of the Fine Arts, 1938, number 22 (reproduced on the brochure cover); reproduced on the 1942 Calendar of the Association of Chicago Painters and Sculptors; Hackley Art Gallery (one-person exhibition), 1967.

25. **CHICAGO RIVER INDUSTRIAL SCENE, c. 1930s**
size: 40" x 50"
signed: lower left
oil on canvas

26. CHICAGO RIVER SCENE, c. 1930s
size: 32" x 36"
signed: lower right
oil on canvas
The Bridges Collection

Exhibited in one-person exhibition at the Drake Hotel, sponsored by the All-Illinois Society of the Fine Arts, 1938, number 13.

27. CHICAGO WORLD'S FAIR, 1933
size: 24-1/2" x 30"
signed: lower left
oil on canvas
Collection of Harlan J. and Pamela M. Berk

28. GALENA, ILLINOIS, c. late 1930s
size: 30" x 36"
signed: lower right
oil on canvas

29. MIDWEST BACKYARDS, c. 1938
size: 30" x 36"
signed: lower right
oil on canvas

Exhibited at Hackley Art Gallery (one-person exhibition), 1967.

30. COUNTRY TRAIN STATION
size: 20" x 24"
signed: lower left
oil on canvas

31. MIDWEST LANDSCAPE WITH STORM
size: 30" x 36"
signed: lower right
oil on canvas

32. CHICAGO FISHING SCENE
size: 32" x 36"
signed: lower left
oil on canvas

33. RAINY DAY, before 1938
size: 26" x 30"
signed: lower left
oil on canvas

Exhibited in a one-person exhibition at the Drake Hotel, sponsored by the All-Illinois Society of the Fine Arts, 1938, number 30; Hackley Art Gallery (one-person exhibition), 1967.

34. BURNING CIGARETTE, before 1938
size: 26" x 30"
signed: lower right
oil on canvas

Exhibited in a one-person exhibition at the Drake Hotel, sponsored by the All-Illinois Society of the Fine Arts, 1938, number 8; Hackley Art Gallery (one-person exhibition), 1967.

35. HOUSE ON OAKENWALD
size: 27" x 20"
signed: lower right
oil on canvas

36. SNOW IN CHICAGO ALLEY, before 1949
size: 30" x 25"
signed: lower right
oil on canvas

37. APPLE TREE
size: 28" x 36"
signed: lower right
acrylic on masonite

38. AN OLD TREE
size: 30" x 24"
signed: lower right
oil on canvas

39. HEAVY SNOW, c. late 1950s
size: 26" x 20"
signed: lower right
oil on canvas

**40. DEMOLITION IN HYDE PARK,
c. late 1950s**
size: 30" x 25"
signed: lower right
oil on canvas
Promised gift of Angenita J. Morris to the
Muskegon Museum of Art

*Exhibited in a one-person exhibition, Chicago Public Library,
1961; Hackley Art Gallery (one-person exhibition), 1967.*

**41. ARRANGEMENT ON A MARBLE
COUNTER**
size: 36" x 32"
signed: lower left
oil on canvas

**42. ANGENITA WITH DOLL,
c. late 1920s**
size: 16" x 11"
signed: lower right
oil on board

43. THE JAPANESE VASE, c. 1931
size: 36" x 32"
signed: lower right
oil on canvas

*Exhibited at the Hackley Art Gallery (one-person exhibition),
1931; Chicago Galleries Association, ca. 1934*

44. STILL LIFE WITH SANSEVIERIA
size: 30" x 24"
signed: lower left
oil on canvas

**45. RED DROP LEAF TABLE WITH
BOTTLES, c. 1950s**
size: 20" x 26"
signed: lower right
oil on canvas

**46. ROOM WITH RED DROP LEAF
TABLE, c. 1950s**
size: 31" x 25"
signed: lower left
oil on canvas

47. AN OPEN DOOR, c. 1950s
size: 26" x 18"
signed: lower left
oil on canvas

**48. VIEW OF CHICAGO THROUGH
BIRCH TREES, c. 1960s**
size: 30" x 24"
signed: lower right
acrylic on board

**49. SUNBEAMS THROUGH THE
CLOUDS, c. 1960s**
size: 40" x 32"
signed: lower right
acrylic on board

50. ABSTRACT, c. 1960s
size: 40" x 32"
signed: lower right
acrylic on board

51. SELF PORTRAIT, 1964
size: 30" x 24"
signed: lower right
oil on canvas

THE ARTIST'S INTENT: THE CONSERVATION OF THE TUNIS PONSEN EXHIBIT

BY KENNETH B. KATZ

FELLOW OF THE INTERNATIONAL INSTITUTE

FOR CONSERVATION

The conservation of a large collection of paintings by the same artist is a unique experience and thrill for any conservator. It is hoped that our efforts reflect kindly on Tunis Ponsen's works and allow the viewer to truly appreciate the legacy of his *oevre*.

From the moment the final application of paint is brushed on to the canvas by any artist, the appearance of the painting changes. The medium begins to dry. A frame is attached, changing the visual boundaries. A varnish is applied that alters the characteristics of the paint, or the artist changes his mind and re-works a section. Beyond these obstructive human elements – to say nothing of obvious distresses such as a bump, a tear or a bulge – the effects of aging alter the character of a painting. Later on in a painting's life, age takes over in the areas not seen by the eye that lie below in layers of canvas, sizings, and underpaints. Cracks appear in the top layers of paint (fig. 33) that were ill prepared by the artist, or appear in areas of paint that have grown brittle and have lost their ability to flex with the movement of the canvas. Applications of varnish begin to yellow, causing once pastel blues to become green, and whites to lose their vibrancy. Grime embeds itself in slow drying surface coatings, flattening out the perspective and casting a grey tone over the work.

Sometimes this is the artist's wish; more often than not, these evitabilities of age change the artist's original intention. If age does not alter the painted image, there is always human intervention, be it the artist, framer, restorer, or conservator. When a painting is displayed, it presents its own history, although sometimes disguised. This masquerade of surface appearance is what the viewer sees and takes note of.

It is the role of the painting conservator, in conjunction with the art historian, to determine the artist's original intentions and to treat the insecurities and disfiguring signs of age that lead away from them. As a guide, we have Ponsen's writings; but most of all, we have a large body of work that has been kept together. By examining his paintings in the studio and comparing them from one period to the other, the conservator can assess their structural and visual condition so as to make treatment recommendations that will result in paintings true to the artist's original intent. As you will see, this intent can, and does, vary during the artist's stylistic periods.

The collected works of Tunis Ponsen exhibited certain general characteristics particular to the time at which they were painted. His early Chicago period, as seen in the *Young Man with Violin* (cat. #3), *Man Holding a Bottle*(cat. #5), and *Male Model* (cat. #1), reflected the use of thick paint, re-working, and wet into wet glazing that, in many instances, resulted in insecure paint. (This period of painting appears to have been influenced by a more classical approach to painting as seen by the Dusseldorf School and American School of Chase and Sargent.) His apparent use of a very slow drying varnish resulted in embedded grime. Furthermore, much of that varnish has yellowed with time.

The work produced after his travels to Europe, as seen in *Barges on the Seine* (cat. #21), *Yacht Club Pier* (cat. #11) and the Gloucester paintings, reflects the impressionistic motif of pure colors and less glazing. One sees a more direct approach and lighter palette as compared to his earlier use of dark and rich glazes laid one upon the other. Nevertheless, these later paintings were also varnished, likely by him, which resulted in their yellowed appearances. Structurally, however, they remained in somewhat better condition. It is also noted at this time that Ponsen himself did restorations or changed the composition, an important factor which had to be taken into account during the present conservation recommendations.

During the forties, Ponsen's style appears to have matured. His paintings are more stable and appear to have been painted technically better. This is especially apparent in his still lifes. Finally in his later period, he began to use acrylic paint on Masonite. These paintings have changed little, but the supports on which they were painted have warped.

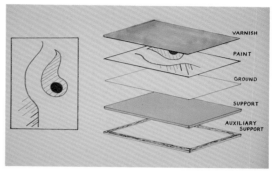

Fig. 33 – Schematic cross-section of painting illustrating different strata.

Fig. 34 – Illustration of paint flowing over age crack indicating overpainting.

Fig. 35 – Photograph taken under ultraviolet light illustrating the blue-green fluorescence of the original varnish and design (top portion of photo), covered up by recent restorations that appear dark (bottom of photo).

Fig. 36 – Detail of overpaint removal corresponding to ultraviolet photograph.

Fig. 37 – Before of *Young Man with Violin*.

With an understanding of the artist's style and intent in a given period, the conservator can address the physical conditions and provide appropriate conservation treatment for an exhibition such as this.

The *Young Man with Violin*, painted in 1924-25, was examined prior to treatment. Examination revealed losses of paint with re-touchings flowing into them (fig. 34), indicating that the original paint was insecure at one time and that someone had applied paint over the loss. The painting had a new canvas attached to the reverse, a procedure called lining, which indicated prior restorative treatments. Research revealed that the painting had been treated in 1972, four years after Ponsen's death. This helped determine that the re-touchings were not his. Tests indicated that the varnish of 1972 had yellowed significantly and there were wholesale restorations in the background. It was decided to remove the restorations.

The removal of the restorations in the background revealed a layer of original yellowed varnish, which confirmed that the paint being removed had been applied over a varnish that had been on long enough to yellow with age (anywhere from 15 to 50 years). This varnish, as all natural resin varnishes, fluoresced blue-green under ultraviolet light, which confirmed its age and composition. Overpaint appears very dark or black (figs. 35 and 36). Removal of the restorations and varnishes resulted in a much lighter background with details of a curtain backdrop, rather than an ill-formed shadow (figs. 37 and 38). Proper cleaning and conservation have turned a once-fine painting that had been ill-treated back to a painting that reflected Ponsen's early style.

Yacht Club Pier, Shipyard at Boothbay Harbor, Maine (cat. #14) and *Gloucester Harbor* (cat. #17) all exhibited Ponsen's developing style, which had changed dramatically from his earlier Chicago period. These pictures were painted more directly with brighter colors and exhibited very different stabilities. They had been varnished, probably by the artist. The varnishes had yellowed, obscuring his once-bright colors. Where *Yacht Club Pier* and *Gloucester Harbor* were stable, *Shipyard* exhibited losses and re-touching that appeared to have been applied by Ponsen.

Treatment, which included varnish removal, resulted in brighter, more colorful paintings (figs. 39 and 40). Ponsen's re-touchings, particularly along the left side of *Shipyard* (fig. 41), were left intact because they did not cause any significant disfigurement or distraction.

Furthermore, in *Shipyard*, images of a mast and flag showing through the final design in the middle left center can be seen (fig. 42). These ghostly images, called "pentimenti," emerge as the upper layers of paint become transparent, exposing the artist's "regrets." Compositionally, the conservation treatment resulted in a compromise between pristine work and the artist's own changes. Visually, the changes in brightness were significant due to removal of the yellowed varnish.

The technique of painting wet into wet and changing his composition without allowing lower layers to dry might explain the conditions found in the *Stone Quarry* (cat. #23). Many areas of thin paint applied on the surface were peeling away from lower areas. In many cases, they covered old losses and cracks. Further, many of these areas were of colors that did not match the surrounding paint. Treatment included injecting adhesive into all the areas of insecurity and lining the painting to reduce movement, which appeared to exacerbate the insecure paint. It was decided to overpaint any areas that were distracting, especially in the mound of snow, and leave areas that were not, particularly in the lower left foreground (figs. 43 and 44). The paint used was reversible; but it was felt that the previous restorations, even if by Ponsen, distracted from the overall enjoyment of the painting. (The assumption that it was Ponsen who applied the overpaint was based on an observation that the application and texture appeared to be similar to his

Fig. 38 – Final photograph of *Young Man with Violin.*

Fig. 39 – During varnish removal of *Yacht Club Pier.*

Fig. 40 – During varnish removal of *Gloucester Harbor.*

Fig. 41 – Ponsen's restoration along left side of water in *Shipyard at Boothbay Harbor, Maine.*

Fig. 42 – Pentimenti of mast.

Fig. 43 – Before of *Stone Quarry.*

techniques. Also, it would be hard to imagine that anybody else would have overpainted so boldly without regard to any original design.)

As part of Ponsen's obvious penchant for restoration, many of his paintings had been structurally treated to prolong their longevity. He had placed bandage tape under the tacking margins and corners to reinforce them during stretching. Some paintings had cardboard placed behind the painting between the stretcher for protection (fig. 45). We start to see many of these techniques in the paintings of the 40s, when his approach appears to have matured. These rudimentary techniques anticipated the treatments of strip lining and attaching backing boards to the reverse of the stretcher.

Structually, little can be said of his later works. His style became somewhat abstract, and his materials changed to acrylics on Masonite (*View of Chicago Through Birch Trees,* cat. #48; *Sunbeams Through the Clouds,* cat. #49; *Abstract,* cat. #50), possibly in the hopes of a more stable product. Today, the colors are fine, but the Masonite has warped.

One aspect of the overall conservation project was to do as little as possible to the paintings, but at the same time, make them safe for travel. To that end, many paintings had polyester fabric attached to the edges (strip lining) and were re-stretched onto their original stretchers. As a result, a few draws (puckers) may ensue, but the integrity of the original painting is only moderately compromised. All paintings had backing board attached and were framed using mending plates rather than nails. Additionally, in keeping with what appears to have been Ponsen's practice of varnishing, all paintings were varnished with synthetic resins that, hopefully, will not yellow. The amount of varnish varied with his period: thicker, glossier varnishes on his earlier works and thinner, not as noticeable sprays on his middle and later works. The amount was determined by what the painting had on it originally.

Only one painting, *View of Chicago Through Birch Trees* did not have the yellowed varnish removed because the pigments below were sensitive to the solvents needed to remove it. This may have been caused by premature varnishing which allowed the varnish to become part of the not fully dried underlayer of paint.

The task of treating an exhibition like this involved many members of the staff at Conservation and Museum Services. Without the help of Diane Barone, Lonore Flores, Nancy Rattenbury, Venus Kwiecinski, and Conservator Renate Jaruseviciute, the timely completion and execution of our responsibilities could not have taken place. Stepping back from our intimate involvement to enjoy the whole of the paintings, not just parts, has rewarded our eyes with images that were meant to be lived with and appreciated over time. *The Lost Paintings of Tunis Ponsen* visitor may concur or disagree with our views. Whatever the views may be, we are confident that they will be based on the artist's intended images, undisguised by time or man.

– K.B.K

Fig. 44 – Final of *Stone Quarry*.

Fig. 45 – Backing board by Ponsen.

CREDITS

FIGURE ILLUSTRATIONS

Unless otherwise noted, all archival materials are courtesy of Angenita J. Morris

Figure 1   Raymond Jonson (1891-1982)
The Night, Chicago, 1921
Courtesy of a private collection

Figure 2   Anthony Angarola (1893-1929)
Michigan Avenue Bridge
Courtesy of ACA Galleries
New York/Munich

Figure 3   Ramon Shiva (1893-1963)
Chicago MCMXXIV, 1924
Courtesy of Harlan J. and Pamela M. Berk

Figure 4   Emil Armin (1883-1971)
The Open Bridge
Courtesy, Illinois State Museum

Figure 5   John Steuart Curry (1897-1946)
Wisconsin Landscape, 1938-39
Courtesy of the Metropolitan Museum
of Art, New York

Figure 6   George Oberteuffer's class
School of the Art Institute, Chicago
Archival material

Figure 7   Students painting, Provincetown,
Massachusetts, 1926
Archival material

Figure 8   Tunis Ponsen
An Old Pier, c. 1929
Purchased by popular subscription
Courtesy of Flint Institute of Arts
Flint, Michigan

Figure 9   Tunis Ponsen
Low Tide, c. 1939
Photograph by Susan Weininger

Figure 10   Tunis Ponsen
An Overmantel: Decorative Paintings, 1928
Photograph from Ponsen archival material

Figure 11   Tunis Ponsen
              Windmill, c. 1928
              Whereabouts unknown

Figure 12   Tunis Ponsen
              Fishing on the Seine, c. 1928

Figure 13   Johan Barthold Jongkind (1819-1891)
              View of Notre Dame, Paris, 1864
              Courtesy of Ashmolean Museum
              Oxford, England

Figure 14   Jean Crawford Adams (1890-1971)
              View from the Auditorium
              Courtesy of Chicago Historical Society

Figure 15   Belle Baranceanu (1902-1988)
              Factory by the River, c. 1930
              Courtesy of Sandra and Bram Dijkstra

Figure 16   Richard Chase
              The City at Night, ca. 1930
              Courtesy of Phil and Janet Graff, Chicago

Figure 17   Todros Geller (c. 1889-1949)
              Michigan Avenue Bridge, 1930
              Courtesy of Richard L. Silverman

Figure 18   Jean Crawford Adams (1890-1971)
              World's Fair Chicago, c. 1933
              Courtesy of David and Mary Winton Green

Figure 19   Emil Armin (1883-1971)
              The Fair and Fishing, c. 1934
              Courtesy, Illinois State Museum

Figure 20   William Schwartz (1896-1977)
              Untitled (City Street), c. 1938
              Courtesy of a private collection

Figure 21   Aaron Bohrod (1907-1992)
              Waiting for the 3:30, 1941
              Courtesy of the Harry S. Truman Library

Figure 22   Demolition site in Hyde Park, 1957
              Archival material

Figure 23   Getrude Abercrombie (1909-1977)
              Doors (3-Demolition), 1957
              Courtesy of the David and Alfred Smart
              Museum of Art, University of Chicago
              Gift of the Gertrude Abercrombie Trust

Figure 24   Painting by Tunis Ponsen, age 14
              Archival material

Figure 25   Ponsen enlists in American army
              Archival material

Figure 26   Ponsen and Angenita
              Archival material

Figure 27   Ponsen business card
              Archival material

Figure 28   Tunis Ponsen
              School of the Art Institute of Chicago
              Graduation portrait, 1925

Figure 29   Tunis Ponsen
              Watercolor study for cat. #39

Figure 30   Tunis Ponsen
              Watercolor study for cat. #22

Figure 31   Ponsen painting at the farm
              Archival material

Figure 32   Tunis Ponsen, age 70
              Archival material

Figures 33-45 These figures accompany the conservation
              analysis and are captioned where they
              appear. Photography by Kenneth B. Katz.

COLOR PLATES

Photography by:

Paul Kooney   Cat. #1, 3-10, 12-41, 43-51

Larry Dikeman Cat. #2, 11, 42; Figs. #29, 30

Contributing Authors

WILLIAM H. GERDTS is Professor of Art History at the Graduate School of the City University of New York. He received his Bachelor of Arts degree from Amherst College and his Master's and Ph.D degrees from Harvard University. He was Curator of Art at the Norfolk Museum, before serving for twelve years as the Curator of Painting and Sculpture at the Newark Museum. He was Associate Professor of Art and Gallery Director at the University of Maryland, before assuming his present position with the City University of New York. A member of the Salmagundi Club, he is on the board of *The American Art Journal*, *The American Art Review*, the International Foundation for Art Research and the Archives of American Art. He is the author of numerous exhibition catalogues and articles in such magazines as *Antiques, The Art Quarterly, Art in America* and others. He is the author of 16 books including *The Drawings of Joseph Stella, American Still-Life Painting, American Neoclassic Sculpture, American Impressionism,* and *Grand Illusions: History Painting in America.* Latest major publications: *Art Across America,* 1990, and the principal essay in *Lasting Impressions: American Painters in France, 1865-1915;* and *Monet's Giverny,* 1993.

PATRICK COFFEY has been a collector, appraiser and lecturer on American art for more than twenty years. He received a B.A. degree from the University of Notre Dame and later studied art history at Wayne State University. Coffey is a former member of the board of directors of the Associates of the American Wing, Detroit Institute of Arts. He has been a member of the Appraisers Association of America, New York, since 1974 and was certified by them as an expert appraiser of American art in 1990. Coffey joined Citizens Insurance Company in 1975 and was elected Vice President–Marketing in 1991.

SUSAN S. WEININGER is Associate Professor of Art History and Assistant Director of the School of Liberal Studies at Roosevelt University, Chicago. She has written, curated exhibitions and lectured extensively on art in Chicago before 1945. This work includes catalogues for the exhibitions of work by *Gertrude Abercrombie* (Illinois State Museum), *Herman Menzel: A Rediscovered Regionalist* (Chicago Historical Society), *The 'New Woman' in Chicago* (Rockford College Gallery) and curating the exhibition *'Thinking Modern': Painting in Chicago, 1910-45* (Mary and Leigh Block Gallery, Northwestern University), for which the catalogue is forthcoming.

KENNETH B. KATZ, Conservator of Historic and Artistic Works of Art earned an M.A. and Advanced Certificate of Training from the Cooperstown Graduate Program of the State University of New York at Oneonta. He established Conservation and Museum Services in Detroit in 1989, following professional experience at the San Francisco Museum of Modern Art, the Minneapolis Institute of Art, the Kimbell Art Museum, Intermuseum Conservation Laboratory in Oberlin, Ohio and the Conversation Laboratory of the Detroit Institute of Arts. Katz was elected Fellow of the International Institute of Conservation in 1990; presently, the only Painting Fellow in Michigan. Recently, Katz served as a conservator on the Michigan State Capitol restoration which included treatment of the Governors' portraits. In addition to the conservation for the Ponsen exhibition, Katz treats fine art paintings for Michigan museums, corporations and private collections.

A MESSAGE FROM
CITIZENS INSURANCE COMPANY
OF AMERICA

While a necessity of life for most people and businesses, property-casualty insurance does not often touch the soul of society or arouse the human spirit. Ethos and pathos are the expressions of more artistic enterprises, which Citizens Insurance Company of America has gladly supported over the past many years. We are especially proud of our collaboration with the Muskegon Museum of Art in the exhibition of "The Lost Paintings of Tunis Ponsen." For what was, initially, a fairly routine review of a homeowners policy application became the rare privilege of rediscovering an important regional artist. Citizens is excited that insurance could play such a revealing role in this production, and we are grateful for the museum's willingness to share this discovery with the public. Certainly, Mr. Ponsen would appreciate having his work shown again at the institution which encouraged his early success and which does so much to encourage the public's appreciation of art today.

TUNIS PONSEN